Aɴchors
For The
Soul

Trusting
GOD
In The
Storms
Of Life

John Mark Hicks

Cover design by Brett Lyerla

International Standard Book Number 0-89900-897-6

CONTENTS

2000 AND BEYOND
STUDIES FOR SMALL GROUPS

In pursuit of our stated goal, "Every Christian a Bible Student," College Press has, since 1995, been publishing a series of *Studies for Small Groups*. These have proved very popular, both for group and individual study on a variety of topics and Scripture texts. Although, with the year 2000, we have changed the outward appearance of these study booklets, our commitment is still to providing solid, thought-provoking studies that will make a life-changing difference in the reader.

Of course, although we call these studies "for small groups," they are equally suited for individual study. If you are simply reading the book for your own benefit, please do take the time to use the "Reflecting on . . ." questions to focus your own thoughts. In a small group study, the questions should not only be used as a review, to see if you remember what was actually said in that lesson by the writer, but to help spark discussion of the further *implications* of the lesson material. Nor should you consider the questions that are provided the only questions to be asked. Any study is only as good as the effort you put into it, and the group leader should have read the lesson through thoroughly before the class meets, as well as encouraging all other members of the group to do so if possible. If the leader has gone through the lesson in advance, he or she will probably have thought of other questions, some of which may never have even occurred to the writer or editors of the study. After all, what is important is not just the bare facts of the lesson, but how they intersect with your own path in the Christian walk.

Above all, do not feel you have to race through the lessons. Although the number of lessons is purposely kept small so that no one has to commit in advance to an endless period of time on the study, you should not cut off discussion of an important issue just to fit the whole of the lesson into one study session. Nor do you want to leave off the end of a lesson because you didn't get it all in during the allotted time. The greatest advantage of the small group setting is the flexibility you have, allowing you to carry over discussion to the next session. Take full advantage of this flexibility.

ANCHORS FOR THE SOUL
TRUSTING GOD IN THE STORMS OF LIFE

"When Job's three friends, Eliphaz the Temanite, Bildad the Shuhite and Zophar the Naamathite, heard about all the troubles that had come upon him, they set out from their homes and met together by agreement to go and sympathize with him and comfort him. When they saw him from a distance, they could hardly recognize him; they began to weep aloud, and they tore their robes and sprinkled dust on their heads. Then they sat on the ground with him for seven days and seven nights. No one said a word to him, because they saw how great his suffering was."

—Job 2:11-13

When Job's friends heard about his plight, they visited Job. Their intention was benevolent. They came to "sympathize with him and comfort him" (Job 2:11). The same Hebrew words (though translated differently) are used again in the epilogue where his friends and relatives "comforted and consoled him over all the trouble the Lord had brought upon him" (Job 42:11).

Their genuine sympathy for Job is expressed in a traditional Near Eastern manner (Job 2:11). They not only raised a great lament with loud cries, they also tore their clothes and threw dust on their heads. Job's reaction to his trouble was similar (Job 1:20). They sat with Job on the trash heap for seven days in silence (Job 2:13). Their friendship could not have been demonstrated more appropriately. Often it is better to be silent in the face of another's suffering than to attempt to soothe their pain with words. Now Job was no longer alone. His friends were with him. "Finally," Job might have thought to himself, "I have someone who will share my pain with me and provide a comforting presence." But Job, and the reader, soon discover that the friends are "miserable comforters" (Job 16:2).

Community is important in suffering. The help of friends is immeasurable. But suffering can also destroy community. In the midst of suffering, humans tend to seek their own interest. We want to preserve our own theology in a way that evidences the basic selfishness of the fallen human spirit. Job rose above this basic inclination to selfishness when he maintained his integrity. But his friends did not. They counseled a false self-incrimination. They sought to preserve their theology by questioning Job's integrity. They cut Job loose from their community because God, in their view, had judged him. Job was without a community.

We moderns are no different. Recently, a minister discovered he was HIV positive through a past blood transfusion. He disclosed this to his congregation and the congregation fired him. What was once a loving community turned on him when they believed that God had judged him for some secret sin. The theology of Job's friends is alive and well.

The dialogue in Job is as much about the destruction of community as it is about bad theology. The reader, who evaluates the dialogue from the standpoint of the narrative prologue (Job 1–2), sees the tragedy of both. The friends model Satan's approach to suffering. Indeed, they are yet another Satanic attempt to destroy Job's faith. His wife counseled Job to maintain his integrity and curse God's injustice. The friends counsel Job to deny his integrity and submit to their version of God's justice. Either way, Satan wins. Job's wife serves God only when he blesses. The friends serve God so that he will bless. In the end, both serve God for profit. But Job rejects both alternatives. Instead, he worships, laments, and trusts (Job 1:20-22; 7:11-21; 23:10-12). He will serve God even when there is no discernible "profit" (Job 21:14-16). He will serve God because there is no one else to trust but God.

In the face of tragedy, the community of God "talks with each other" about the fear of the Lord (Mal. 3:13-18). The Lord listens, remembers, and he will one day redeem his people as his own possession. One day redemption will overcome tragedy, and grief will give way to joy. But as the community waits for that day, how does it "talk with each other"? What does the community of faith say, for example, to those who have experienced the tragic death of a child? What do we say to sufferers? How do we avoid the mistakes of Job's friends? What should we say? What can we say?

This study booklet is the practical conclusion of my larger 300-page book entitled *Yet Will I Trust Him: Understanding God in a Suffering World* (Joplin, MO: College Press, 1999). Much of the material in this booklet is adapted from its first and last chapters. I hope that presenting the material in this form will enable churches and small group Bible studies to think with me through some of these grand biblical themes that help sufferers and offer comfort.

I am sometimes asked, "What helps you endure your trials? What gets you through the tough times?" The full answer to those questions involves the theological story that I tried to tell in the above-mentioned book. I will take a brief aside in the first three lessons to introduce the discussion in lessons four through eight.

I think the theological story boils down to five simple but profound theological *anchors*. These five principles summarize the story and anchor faith. When the waves of doubt and despair assail, I often reflect on these five points. They provide a foundation and, through the Spirit of God, they empower whatever endurance I might have. These five theological truths are anchors for the soul during the storms of life.

A PERSONAL STORY

In this lesson:

> ▶ Learning suffering firsthand
> ▶ The benefits of faithful lament
> ▶ The difference between joy without lament and joy with lament

Men cry out under a load of oppression,
they plead for relief from the arm of the powerful.
But no one says, "Where is God my Maker,
who gives songs in the night? "

—Elihu to Job, Job 35:9-10

On May 22, 1977, I married. I was young, only nineteen, and even though I had already earned a B.A. degree in Religion at a private Christian college, I was incredibly naive about the world's evil and pain. I had not experienced the pain of personal suffering, nor had my understanding of God been radically challenged. Suffering, I thought, does not come from God — only good.

However, in 1980 this vision was shaken. My innocence was shattered, and my naïve, simplistic belief in God's providential goodness was tested. On April 30, 1980, Sheila, my wife of less than three years, died suddenly and unexpectedly at home while recovering from surgery when a blood clot stopped her heart.

We had hoped for children in the near future. In fact, Sheila underwent back surgery so she could carry a child full term. We had planned to pursue a missionary career in Germany where we hoped to minister in the eastern block. We had planned, prayed, and pursued so much, but on April 30, 1980 all those dreams were dashed. The pillars of my faith were shaken by her death and cracks began to emerge. Had we not dedicated ourselves to God's service? Had we not prayed for health and protection? Why had God not empowered us for ministry in Germany? Why had God not preserved the life of my spouse? Where were his blessings now? Why would he not spare her life?

I renewed my study of Scripture. Could Scripture speak to the aching heart? In particular, I studied Psalms, Job, and Ecclesiastes. I re-read the narratives of God's story. It was as if I had never read that literature before — and, in a very real sense, I had not. Before my suffering I could never empathize with Job. Before my suffering I could never understand the intense emotions of the psalmists. Now, I too, had suffered, and it opened up the possibilities of an empathetic reading of Scripture. This renewed reading opened up a world I never knew existed. I discovered that one can read accounts of suffering empathetically only if one has already suffered. No amount of textbook exposure can generate that genuine empathy.

FAITHFUL LAMENT

At one point I can remember believing that such a world of suffering could not exist in the believer's life. I remember thinking that the world is God's good creation, God is good, and therefore I should expect good, especially in the light of the resurrection of Jesus. There is no room for despair in a world where God has dispelled it through Jesus Christ. We should always rejoice and never lament. Christians should always wear a smile. However, through an empathetic reading of Psalms, Job, and other parts of Scripture, I entered a new world, the world of *faithful lament.*

Faithful lament was a new category for me. How can lament, with its accusations, bewilderment, doubt, tears, and frustrations, express faith? Prior to my own personal suffering, lament was unknown to me. Christianity was a faith of joy, celebration, and hopeful anticipation. Life taught me to rejoice, look forward to the future, and celebrate God's victory through ministry.

> Through an empathetic reading of Psalms, Job, and other parts of Scripture, I entered a new world, the world of faithful lament.

My worldview was dominated by that triumphalism. God's army will conquer. We will set the world aright. We will establish the perfect church. My outlook had no room for lament (and little room for failure) since such would accuse God or fault him for suffering. But my own suffering forced me to lament because the believer, who continues to believe, can only lament in the midst of suffering. Lament expresses the sufferer's faith. Lament does not disown God; it appeals to him. It calls upon God to do something, to help, to rescue the one who has been faithful to him. It cries "my God."

BENEFICIAL SUFFERING

By God's grace, however, those early years of lament turned to praise because God renewed my joy through Barbara, whom I married in November of 1983. Our union included a fifteen-month-old ball of fire named Ashley. She has always filled our home with love, excitement, and unpredictability. In 1985 God blessed us with a son whom we named Joshua in order to give him a vision for how he might one day serve God like Joshua of old. In 1987 God blessed us with another beautiful girl, Rachel. The biblical name reflected our prayer that God would use her in his service as well. During these times of divine refreshing God blessed me. He fulfilled my dreams, hopes, and expectations. My family and my ministry were my joys. Suffering seemed a thing of the past. Yet, even as I gave credit to God for the joys of my new family, I still wondered about the meaning of the suffering I had endured. Should God get credit for that as well?

> I still wondered about the meaning of the suffering I had endured. Should God get credit for that as well?

As I now look back upon the suffering of my youth, I must admit that a genuine sense of gratitude arises within me. It may sound harsh, but I confess with the psalmist that "it was good for me to be afflicted" (Ps. 119:71). Of course, affliction is never good in an absolute sense (death is God's enemy), but sometimes it is good in a relative sense. The relative good of his suffering, according to this psalmist, is related to the waywardness of his life prior to his affliction. He wrote: "Before I was afflicted I went astray, but now I obey your word" (Ps. 119:67). While all suffering cannot be so categorized (as, for example, in the case of Job), I identify with the psalmist's perspective. God afflicted me in faithfulness (Ps. 119:75).

Sheila and I were planning to spend several years on the mission field, but in my heart I was also planning to study there and return to the States triumphantly. I would have a European Ph.D. in one hand and the glory of missionary experience in the other. I thought no Christian college would deny me the opportunity to teach. I was arrogant in my theology — I knew what was right, preached maliciously against error, and chastened everyone who left the "old paths" of my tradition. I had sided with the right wing of my heritage, and was closely associated with an editor, lecturer, and publisher who epitomized it. He published me and I invited him for speaking engagements. My spirit was contentious, my attitude was arrogant, my theology was perfect, and my goal was selfish. Of course, at the time, I would never have admitted these things. Indeed, I did not understand them about myself, and probably very few, if any, recognized them in me. I did not see myself for what I really was. Youth has its many blind spots. I know my 22-year-old self better now than I did then. Hindsight is always better. I can see now where I would have ended up had something not happened to change my direction.

> God changed me as I experienced his comforting presence and transforming power through suffering.

Sheila's death changed me. Scripture changed me. My encounter with the God of Scripture changed me. God changed me as I experienced his comforting presence and transforming power through suffering. The effect of that change was such that whereas I once had God so pegged that I knew what to expect from him and could plan out the course of my life without interruption, I now realized that my attitude must be one of submission. Humility must replace arrogance, submission must replace pride, and gentleness must replace contentiousness. In other words, God's glory must replace my selfishness. Without that experience — at that moment — my heart may have hardened, and my path may have been set.

God used Sheila's death to change me. But was that fair? Why should Sheila suffer for my good? Why her instead of me? I was the problem, not her! I was filled with pride, but she was not. I wanted to move up the "hierarchical" ladder of my church, but she just wanted to serve God. I wanted to be noticed, but that did not consume her. Why her instead of me? These questions have often plagued me. They are difficult questions, but in lament faith asks. But no matter how they are answered, I thank God for the change he worked in my life. Through my suffering — whatever the origin and reason for that suffering — God worked powerfully to effect good in my life. He opened my heart to his transforming presence.

Despite the questions, I confess with the psalmist that it was good for me to have been afflicted. My sense is that if I had not been tried by suffering, my heart would have continued down its selfish, prideful, and arrogant path. My life would have been very different. Now I praise God for that affliction and I thank him for the change he worked in me. That change came in the context of prayerful lament over Sheila's death. But how can I thank God for the death of one I loved so dearly?

REDEFINED HOPE

Nevertheless, since 1983 I have constantly thanked God for his renewal through Barbara, Ashley, Joshua, and Rachel. However, late in 1990 lament again entered my life. Joshua had always been a strong, strapping, and energetic boy. He was hyperactive and always getting into trouble. He enjoyed breaking things, was constantly disruptive, and was quickly expelled from the 4K program of a local Baptist church. Even though his behavior was never malicious, for a time we thought we would spend our twilight years visiting him at San Quentin.

We knew we had a problem. Joshua was developing slowly, and he was extremely aggressive. He never said more than one sentence at a time, and his sentences were never more than four or five words. He could never color within the lines, never learned the alphabet, and could rarely do anything that other four and five-year-olds could do. He was developmentally delayed and socially dysfunctional.

We began to seek remedies. We doubted our parenting skills and sought help. We took Joshua to a child psychologist. We tried

> We doubted our parenting skills and sought help.

drugs for hyperactivity. Nothing seemed to work. Instead of progressing, Joshua began to regress. He began to lose what communication skills he had. He returned to wearing diapers, and his aggressiveness increased.

Eventually, we took him to a pediatric neurologist. He immediately recognized a genetic condition. That day we discovered that our son would never get better, and in the first few months of 1991 we learned that his genetic condition was terminal.

Joshua has Mucopolysaccharidosis IIIA (Sanfilippo Syndrome A) which is a genetic storage disorder. He is missing an enzyme that breaks down storage. The condition destroys the brain and debilitates the body. The prognosis was that Joshua would probably leave us sometime before his sixteenth birthday after a slow mental and physical degeneration.

Joshua is now sixteen. He can no longer communicate verbally. He cannot walk or stand by his own strength. His mental age is about six months. He wears diapers. He is bedridden. He will die a lingering death unless his heart or liver problems or pneumonia takes him first. We do not expect him to live through the summer of 2001.

Suffering has again entered my life and the life of my family. It has attacked one of my children. And once again, I identify with Job. His children were his joy, his spiritual concern, and his investment in the future, but he lost them in his suffering. Now my joy, my investment in the future, is gone; my only son will soon die. He will not be the leader among God's people as we had hoped. He will not play baseball, or ever again say the words "I love you."

But this time my perspective is different. Suffering is not a new experience for me, even though each experience of suffering is new. The hopes we invested in our son when we named him have been dashed. Our dreams for him as a leader of God's people are gone. Now our greatest joy is hearing him laugh and listening to him coo as we tell him that we love him. Yet, we long to hear him say "I love you" in response. We have accepted his

We have learned how to lament as a family, and we have experienced the anger and depression that comes with grief.

eventual death, but we lament our plight. We have learned how to lament as a family, and we have experienced the anger and depression that comes with grief.

CONCLUSION

I have experienced two kinds of joy: joy without previous lament (life with Sheila) and joy with lament (life with Barbara). Both are God's blessing, especially the joy despite lament. Joy with lament is rooted in the experience of "seeing" God as we sit on the trash heap (see Job 42:5). It is a confidence that comes through experiencing God's presence in the sanctuary (see Ps. 73:17). The Psalms and Job point us to this kind of lament through which God gives songs to the heart. Elihu, as quoted at the beginning of this lesson, pointed Job toward the God "who gives songs in the night" (Job 35:10). God can give joy in the midst of lament. He can give a song of praise in the middle of suffering's darkness. Lament gives way to joy as it gives way to praise. Elihu pointed Job in the right direction. When Job finally "saw" God, he found a song of praise, even during his night of suffering (Job 42:2-6).

> God can give joy in the midst of lament and a song of praise in the middle of suffering's darkness.

Nevertheless, it is still lament. We still question, wonder, despair, cry, and doubt. Lament often turns to praise, but sometimes lament needs to continue to complain, question, and plead. Had we not prayed for Joshua's health? Did we not ask God to raise him up as a leader among his people? Why has God denied us this joy? Why has God denied himself a servant? How can Joshua serve God in the grave?

The questions remain. The laments continue. But there are also "songs in the night" (Job 35:10; Ps. 77:6). How can both exist together? Scripture and experience have taught me that God gives songs of praise to his people who experience the night, but he does it in unexpected and surprising ways.

Reflecting on Lesson One

1. Read Psalm 119:65-88.

    a. Do you see the elements of lament in this section? What questions does the psalmist ask God?

    b. Where does the psalmist find comfort ultimately? For what does he ask?

    c. How is it "good" that the psalmist was afflicted? What did he learn?

2. Does it disturb you to think about the "goodness of affliction"? What can be good about affliction?

3. Does the recognition of that "goodness" dispel its pain and hurt? Why? Why not? In what ways?

4. What do we do when we cannot see any "good" in the affliction? This was the case with Job. How does he model endurance for us when we cannot see any good in the situation?

5. What is your story in relation to suffering? In what ways do you identify with my story and in what ways do you not?

6. How does God give "songs in the night"? Can you share a "song in the night" of your suffering that God gave you?

Consider this:

Think back to a time when you were with someone who was grieving and said or did something really foolish (we've all been there!). Do you know what you should have done differently? If you have ever been in a grieving situation, who was the greatest comfort to you and why? Consider the difference in the two responses and formulate an idea of what might be the best thing to do the next time you are confronted with a grieving friend. Then read lesson two and compare your conclusions to the author's.

2

THE COURAGE OF SILENCE

In this lesson:
▶ The comfort of silence
▶ Lament must be listened to even though it is painful
▶ Doing versus offering

Teach me, and I will be quiet;
show me where I have been wrong.
How painful are honest words!
But what do your arguments prove?
Do you mean to correct what I say,
and treat the words of a despairing man as wind?
You would even cast lots for the fatherless
and barter away your friend.

*But now be so kind as to look at me.
Would I lie to your face?
Relent, do not be unjust;
reconsider, for my integrity is at stake.
Is there any wickedness on my lips?
Can my mouth not discern malice?*

—Job to Eliphaz, Job 6:24-30

Sometimes silence is better than speaking, listening better than advice, and sympathy better than instruction.

We have all had the experience of fumbling for words in the presence of suffering. We visit a family at a funeral home only to leave embarrassed by the inadequacy of the words we spoke. We take food to the home of grieving parents, but we have no confidence in what we said to them. We see a griever at church for the first time and we avoid speaking to her because we do not know what to say.

We feel inadequate as comforters because we do not know what to say. I think this is a healthy sense of inadequacy. Otherwise, we might become arrogant in our attempt to offer comfort. We may actually think we have something to say that resolves the grief and dispels the pain. No comforter can do that though many have tried.

Job's friends tried. But instead of comforting they deepened the pain. They were "miserable comforters" (Job 16:2). They tried to speak, and they worsened the situation instead of helping. Sometimes, unlike Job's friends, we need to have the courage of silence.

ELIPHAZ, THE "COMFORTER," AND JOB, THE SUFFERER

Job's three friends sat with him on the trash heap for seven days in silence (2:11-13). Job broke that silence with a heart-breaking lament in which he cursed the day of his birth (3:1). Eliphaz, displeased with Job's lament, counseled him to confess his sin because trouble comes to the wicked (5:3-7). Indeed, the wicked suffer the kind of trouble that Job has experienced, and God has judged Job (4:5-8). Job's house had been cursed due to his sin (5:3), and Job must now submit to God's discipline (5:17). Job must humble himself, confess his sin, and seek God's mercy so that God might redeem him (5:11). Though God has wounded Job, God may yet heal him if Job repents (5:18). Only when Job humbles himself will God restore his wealth, children, and security (5:24-26). Eliphaz is confident about his advice. "So hear it," he says to Job, "and apply it to yourself" (5:27).

Job is discouraged by Eliphaz's words. Eliphaz has not eased Job's burden, but increased it. Job is struggling to persevere in faith, but Eliphaz accuses him of faithlessness. Job cries out to God for relief through death. Job wants his life to end without denying "the words of the Holy One" (6:9-10). Job is still faithful, but his pain tempts him to deny God. Eliphaz offers no sympathy. On the contrary, he assails Job's integrity and tells him to repent of his hidden sins. Job hoped for comfort from his friends — even "a despairing man should have the devotion of his friends" (6:14). Instead, his friends are like dried up streams (6:15-17) for which caravans hope, but are disappointed when they reach them (6:18-20). His friends are "no help" (6:21).

> Job is struggling to persevere in faith, but Eliphaz accuses him of faithlessness.

Job is willing to listen (6:24-26). Job will be silent if his friends will say something useful. Eliphaz's descriptions of the plight of the wicked were insinuations that Job himself was one of them. Job is willing to listen to any accusations or charges that the friends know. But he wants proof. Job complains that his friends had not really listened to him. His words were honest. They were the words of a person in great distress and despair. But Eliphaz had treated them as if they were nothing but hot air ("wind"). Eliphaz listened to Job's lament in order to critique rather than suffer with him.

Eliphaz's callous response evokes Job's assessment of his heart (6:27). Eliphaz is the kind of person who would gamble over fatherless children or barter away a friendship. Eliphaz is the sort of person who turns every situation to his own advantage. Rather than help a friend, Eliphaz becomes defensive of his own traditions and beliefs. Eliphaz's rebuke is more concerned about his traditions and values than it is about Job's troubles and spiritual health.

> At stake is not the traditions of the friends, but the integrity of Job.

Job gets to the point (6:28-30). The kindness he expects from Eliphaz and his other friends is trust. Job simply wants his friends to believe him. Job is not a liar. He wants to be treated justly and compassionately. What is really at stake in this dialogue is not the traditions of the friends, but the integrity of Job. God affirmed Job's integrity both before and after trouble enveloped him (1:1; 2:3; 42:7). Job does not belong among the wicked. He is a righteous sufferer. As the narrator commented after Job's second trial, "In all this, Job did not sin in what he said" (2:10).

Eliphaz's words did not heal. They opened the wound wider. Job felt attacked rather than comforted. When the friends were silent, Job felt he could lament in front of his friends. He thought they would understand and comfort him. Instead, they rebuked him. Job lost his last comfort when his "comforters" spoke.

THE ACT OF SILENCE

How, then, do we approach sufferers? We should approach them in silence. The advice for a comforter is: "Don't speak." We are often too quick to speak to sufferers. We are uncomfortable with silence, so we feel we must say something. "Do you see a man who speaks in haste? There is more hope for a fool than for him" (Prov. 29:20). A lengthy silence is better than a hasty sentence. Appropriate comfort expresses itself in three forms.

1) *Presence.* But silence is awkward. Silence burdens us so that we feel as if we are not helping. But comfort comes more in the form of presence than words. I do not remember anything anyone said at my wife's funeral. However, I do remember who was there. Oh, well, I do remember some of the well-intentioned but "stupid" things people said. I would have preferred they had been silent. But I understand their awkwardness and have made the same mistakes. But it was more important that they just be there, and I remember their presence even when I do not remember our conversations.

For example, some of my most precious memories of the events surrounding my wife's funeral involve the presence of people. A friend flew in from Oklahoma to be with me. My sister drove me home to Bowling Green, Kentucky, from Georgia. My father walked with me for several hours. I do not remember anything any of these loved ones said to me, but I remember that they gave their time and presence.

Primary comfort for the griever does not come through the words of comforters, but through their presence. The comforter's presence at the funeral home is much more significant than anything they might say. The fact that they sent a card is more significant than anything they wrote in the card. Consequently, it is so important that comforters make every effort to spend time with sufferers from the earliest moments. Presence communicates much more than anything a comforter might say. The first rule of comfort is: be there and be silent.

2) *Listen.* We should approach sufferers as listeners. We should give them permission to speak. We should sit with them in their lament, offer our sympathy, and

> The first rule of comfort is: be there and be silent.

share their tears. Eliphaz was shocked by Job's words. He did not hear Job's anguish. He did not give Job permission to speak his heart and cry out to his God. We must be willing to sit with sufferers and give them permission to speak to God in deep lament with all the doubts, fears, and questions those laments contain. Too often we divert the conversation to mundane topics because we are uncomfortable listening to the grief and pain of another. Comforters must share the pain rather than avoid it. God listens to our laments, and we should listen to each other's.

It is heartrending to listen to a mother talk about her dead child. It is difficult to listen to a young wife talk about her deceased husband. It is painful to listen to the pain of others. But that is the role of a comforter. We do not help the sufferer when we change topics and move the conversation away from grief and pain. We only signal to the griever that we are not willing to listen and that we are not willing to share the pain. When we fail to listen, we become obstructionists rather then comforters.

It is not the comforter's task to lead a discussion but to be a silent listener. But as listeners we must be willing to listen, even when our pain is increased by what we hear. When the griever laments, do not rebuke or chastise. We listen silently, and listen in such a way that it gives the griever permission to speak. When the griever is ready to speak, we should be ready to listen. We must give the griever permission to be angry and to speak to God or about God with bitterness and impatience, just as righteous Job did. We need to give the griever permission to remember and cry. As uncomfortable as it makes us, it is an important aspect of healing for those who are hurting. We are God's instruments of comfort, and just as God listens, so should we.

> As listeners we must be willing to listen, even when our pain is increased by what we hear.

3) *Action.* Comforters are not restricted to passive acts like silence and listening. Indeed, comforters must also take matters into their own hands and act on behalf of the sufferer. They can do something for the sufferer that eases the burden of grief.

Many times comforters divert this call to action by expressing their desire to help. They may say to the sufferer, "If there is anything we can do, please let us know." While this is surely well-intentioned and deeply felt, the sufferer will never ask. In fact, unwittingly, the comforter places a further burden on the sufferer by placing the initiative in their hands. Now the sufferer must decide when it is appropriate to ask, and the sufferer will not ask without feeling guilty. Even when there is such a close relationship between two people that neither would mind asking or being asked, it still places the burden on the sufferer to initiate the action.

I think it is better to just do something. Show up at their house and say,

1) "I am here to mow your grass." Or,

2) "I am here to clean your house." Or,

3) "Here's tonight's dinner."

The sufferer will politely object — we have been trained to do things for ourselves, even grieve alone without help — but the comforter will act nevertheless. I don't know who changed the oil in my car, who paid for a plane ticket, or cleaned my room, but those acts relieved the burden of my grief because it took away some of the worries and turmoils of daily life. One Christian lady regularly announced to my family that she was going to take care of Joshua for an evening and released us to do something together as a family. When my sister's husband died, several ladies were at the house to clean, arrange food, and to facilitate guests. These acts are more comforting than any words anyone could speak.

Action expresses love. It identifies with the sufferer because the comforter thinks as a sufferer and seeks to relieve the burdens of life as much as possible. When we act, we put ourselves into the place of sufferers and see the world with their eyes.

> When we act, we put ourselves into the place of sufferers and see the world with their eyes.

We do things for them they cannot do for themselves, or we do things for them that in the midst of grief are tremendous burdens (e.g., washing clothes, etc.). When we lift their burdens, we express our love and sympathy.

CONCLUSION

What do we say to sufferers? The first thing we say is nothing.

As awkward as it feels, we must have the courage of silence. Otherwise we may make the mistake of Eliphaz or stumble over words that will only be remembered for their stupidity not their comfort. Silence is the first task of the comforter.

But silence is only significant if we are also present. We can be silent at a distance, but this is no comfort. Be silent, but also be there. Be silent, but also be there to listen. Be silent, but also be there to do something to ease the burdens of life.

Reflecting on Lesson Two

1. Why did Job react the way he did to his friend's speech in Job 5? What in Eliphaz's words and attitude hurt him?

2. Why do we feel like we need to say something to sufferers? Why is silence so awkward?

3. Why is it difficult to listen to a sufferer? Why are we uncomfortable with lament?

4. Is it hard to believe that there are such people as "righteous sufferers" in the world? Why did Eliphaz find that hard to believe?

5. What sort of things have people done for you in your times of grief that helped?

6. What do you think about saying, "If there is anything we can do for you, let us know"? When is that appropriate or inappropriate?

7. Do you know someone who is suffering? What can you do this week to help them? Decide to act.

Consider this:

Whether sufferer or comforter, it is human nature to want to understand why. When you have suffered, did you understand why? Do you now? How do you think God wants us to approach this process of understanding why things happen to us? Is it good to know why something happens? Will it make the pain any less, or will it possibly increase the pain?

3

A TIME TO SPEAK

In this lesson:
> ▶ Interpreting events versus simply offering love
> ▶ Six things you should never say to sufferers
> ▶ God's empathetic participation in our pain

I have heard many things like these;
miserable comforters are you all!
Will your long-winded speeches never end?
What ails you that you keep on arguing?
I also could speak like you,
if you were in my place;
I could make fine speeches against you
and shake my head at you.

But my mouth would encourage you;
comfort from my lips would bring you relief.
—Job to his "Friends," Job 16:2-5

A time to speak does come, but we must be very careful about what we say. Job's friends spoke, but they heaped anguish on top of Job's pain. They argued, interpreted, and advised repentance. But Job wanted comfort, not argument. He wanted sympathy, not accusations.

What do we say in the presence of the suffering? Is there anything that is appropriate? Is there anything that can help?

SIMPLY EXPRESS LOVE

When we first see sufferers in the midst of their suffering, if we say anything, we should simply express love and sympathy. The context of tragedy is no place for theological diatribes. It is not a place for interpreting what has happened. It is not a time for bombastic, simplistic, and pithy platitudes. "A fool finds no pleasure in understanding but delights in airing his own opinions" (Prov. 18:2). We should suffer with our friends rather than attempt to restructure their theology or probe their life circumstances so we can offer them a correct understanding of their situation. We should weep with them rather than explain what has happened.

Job's friends made the mistake of correcting Job rather than sharing his suffering. They thought they could explain his suffering, but all Job wanted was someone to share it with him. Instead of helping him, his friends became "miserable comforters" (Job 16:2).

However, when the sufferer speaks and seeks personal engagement with another, the comforter first listens and then speaks. But what do comforters say? Comforters can reinforce the loving relationship that exists between the two; they can express love. Comforters can speak words of sympathy. They might say,

1) "I am so sorry to hear about your loss." Or,

2) "I can't imagine how painful this must be for you; I am so sorry." Or,

3) "I am praying for you, and I want you to know that I love you." Or,

4) "I just wanted you to know that I am thinking of you." Or,

5) just simply, "I love you."

These words do not comment on the situation. They do not interpret. They simply reflect a heart that weeps with the sufferer. They express sympathy, care, and love. That is all sufferers really want to hear, if they want to hear anything. They want to know others care and that others share their grief. To hear much more than that in the midst of pain is often too much to bear.

When we begin to interpret, when we seek to lessen the pain of grief by relativizing it ("it is not so bad"), we fail to sit with sufferers in their mourning. We become outsiders looking in rather than sympathizers sitting with them. If we intimate that there is some interpretation or meaning that relativizes the pain, then we signal that we are no longer fellow-sufferers. We no longer sit with them on the mourning bench, but we have mounted the pulpit.

> When we begin to interpret, we become outsiders looking in rather than sympathizers sitting with them.

THINGS NEVER TO SAY

When in the presence of grieving parents (and other kinds of grief as well), the loss of words is stunning. We do not know what to say, how to say it, or whether to say anything. Indeed, it is often better to say nothing. But there are some things we should *never* say during the trauma of grief.

1) *"This was the will of God."* In the context of grief, this statement is no comfort. Rather, it becomes an accusation against God. It generates anger, doubt, and bitterness. It may be a statement the sufferer can make, but it is not something a comforter should say. It may be that sufferers can have such confidence in God's work in the world that they are able to say this in a way that offers comfort, but when it is offered by a would-be comforter it is counterproductive. It evokes an image that associates God with the horror of a child's death. Should we believe that God could want something so horrible? What do you mean it "was the will of God"? Did God want my child to die? These are questions which the sufferer may ask. But they are questions which the comforter should not raise or answer because in the midst of suffering there is no reasonable answer.

The sufferer will probably never fit the pieces together. This is part of the struggle of suffering itself. It is what opens up our hearts to discover whether we serve God for profit or whether we serve him out of love.

> The sufferer is not helped when told that the death of a child was the will of God.

But it is the struggle that each sufferer must endure, and the sufferer is not helped when told by a would-be comforter that the death of a child was the will of God. Perhaps there will be opportunity to discuss those dimensions of suffering when faith has had time to settle the heart, but in the initial stages of grief these words offer turmoil, not peace.

2) *"God plucked a rose out of his garden."* This is a wonderful metaphor because it pictures God as a concerned gardener. It offers us a serene picture of death — God picking roses out of his garden for his use and display. God has taken them home to enjoy his presence. But in the midst of grief this is a horrible picture of God. The griever does not see this sentimentalism, but rebels against the notion that God stole a rose. God has many roses, why did he pluck mine? God may have plucked this rose, but it was my rose! The griever sees this image more along the lines of a thief than a loving gardener. The griever is not ready to hear this in the midst of grief, and the comforter offers no comfort with such a statement. Rather, it antagonizes the pain of grief and incites further bitterness toward God.

3) *"Some good will come out of this."* What good would justify the death of a child? Would anyone not gladly exchange that good for the life of his or her child? In the midst of suffering, there is no good that is worth the pain of the moment, especially when it is your child that is dead. To raise the hope or the potential that something good can arise out of a child's death is to ask the sufferer to compare the imagined good with the life of their child. In the midst of grief, there is no contest. There is no good that God could achieve that is worth the life of a child. The darkness of suffering does not permit the acknowledgment of a greater good, and even if there is a greater good, the one sitting in dark-

> The darkness of suffering does not permit the acknowledgment of a greater good.

ness cannot see it. That good arises out of suffering may not be questioned — look at the good God accomplished through the death of his own Son — but whether any particular good is worth any particular suffering is always doubted, especially in the initial moments of that suffering.

What is the greater good? Is it simply to change my character for the better? Is that worth the death of my son? In the heart of a sufferer, there is nothing so absolutely good as the life of the child, and so there is no good that could be achieved through the child's death that is worth that price. What good would I exchange for the life of my son? What "good" is worth that price? Perhaps later on, perhaps when the good is perceived as communion with God, the sufferer may see the greater good, but during grief these words reveal to the sufferer that the comforter does not understand the darkness of suffering.

4) *"It was for the best."* How can the death of my son be "for the best"? While this is usually said about those who have suffered intensely or died in their elderly years, it is still an extremely interpretative statement. It may be true, but the comforter is not an interpreter. The comforter should not offer an explanation. Rather, the comforter is there to share the pain and the grief; to rebel against death and complain about its presence in the world. Only God can judge the relative "better" or "best" of a death; only he can judge the relative "good" of a death. Interpretation is best left up to him, and secondarily to the sufferer, but never for the comforter.

5) *"You need to take a hard look at your life. God is telling you something."* These words force sufferers to look into their own hearts for the rationale of their suffering. They may even imply that God is punishing the sufferer, or at least that some character flaw in the sufferer is the reason God permitted a child's

The parent feels responsible and interprets the statement as an accusation.

death. The parent, then, feels responsible and interprets the statement as an accusation. Is there something so wrong with me that God would take my child? Am I to blame for my child's illness? Did God strike my son just to change me, just to make me better?

Is the death of a child really worth the character-shaping value it might produce? In grief, parents do not exalt the value of their own character development above the life of their child. It is an incredulous thought that God should strike a child for the sake of the parent. Perhaps, however, given time, when character development is seen as a means to communion with God, then the sufferer will see what God has taught and value suffering itself.

There may be a sense in which each of these statements is true. I discuss some of the reasons why they may be true in my book, *Yet Will I Trust Him*. But while there is some truth in each of these statements, the grieving parent cannot hear it in the initial moments, even months, perhaps years, of their grief. These truths have an ugly ring in the ears of grieving parents. Consequently, they should not be offered by would-be comforters, even if they are well-intentioned. They sound like superficial platitudes in the midst of suffering.

REMIND THEM GENTLY

The kinds of statements noted above are unhelpful because they interpret the meaning of a child's death. If it is God's will, what did he intend to do through this child's death? What did God want to accomplish? What good could possibly come from the death of children? Is God punishing me? Is God testing me? What does God want me to learn, and is that lesson worth the death of my child? These are all interpretative questions. They seek the meaning of a child's death.

But this quest for meaning cannot be sustained in the midst of grief. Grieving parents need to lament, question, accuse, even doubt. It is not the time for interpretation and introspection. Later, as the initial shock dissipates, the sufferer will reflect on its meaning and purpose. Sufferers will do their own interpreting, and they may ask for help. Only then does the comforter have permission to interpret with them. But ultimately interpretation belongs only to sufferers. And, certainly, the funeral or the initial months is not a time for an outsider to offer an interpretation of the tragedy (much like Job's friends did). Interpretation is best left to sufferers, and then it only comes with hindsight.

The role of the comforter is not to interpret, but to remind. The comforter is present as the instrument of God's presence among those who weep. The comforter is not there to explain, theologize about the meaning of suffering, or to render a judgment about why a child died. Job's friends made that mistake. The comforter is there, well, just to be there. The comforter sits beside the sufferer and shares the suffering. The comforter is there to sit on the mourning bench with the mourner; to share the lament, the protest, and the questions. The comforter is there to pray with the sufferer. Comforters know how to share suffering, to weep with those who weep, and to sit silently with the weeping sufferer.

> The comforter is present as the instrument of God's presence.

But comforters can also remind the sufferer of things that are a bit blurry in the midst of grief. They can remind the sufferer about what is easily forgotten because suffering is so painful. I believe those reminders must focus on who God is, how God feels about tragedy, and what God will one day do about it. I believe we need to remind sufferers that God sits on the mourning bench with them.

> God is the weeping God who hurts for his children, listens to them, and delivers them.

Healing comes to sufferers when they are reminded of who God is, not when we speak as interpreters. We do not have the prophetic insight to interpret God's actions in the world, but we do have the story of God that tells us who God is. God is the weeping God who hurts for his children, listens to them, and delivers them. This is the story of God and it comforts the hurts and pains.

Just as the psalmist said, we must remember God's works, meditate on them and consider their significance (Ps. 77:11-12; 143:5). There, in God's mighty works, we can find comfort. There we come to know our God and trust his care for us.

CONCLUSION

Under appropriate circumstances, I would speak words of remembrance to sufferers. I call them "five anchors for the soul." They are the anchors I want to cultivate in the life of a church. They do not interpret God's work in suffering, but they remind me of who God is and what he has done. They are reminders of God's story. Sufferers need to first remember, and then they may interpret (though only cautiously and tentatively). Comforters must remind, but resist interpretation.

While comforters need to leave the interpretation to the sufferers, these five principles provide a framework for interpretation. They are the lens through which we read our own stories. They are the context in which we should interpret God's work in our lives. But interpretation is a task for the sufferer, not the comforter.

Consequently, these principles, contained in the next five lessons, not only summarize the story of God, but they are also the essence of what I think sufferers need to remember, what comforters need to offer, and what teachers need to provide for their communities in preparation for suffering.

Reflecting on Lesson Three

1. What did Job find so disagreeable about his friends' speeches?

2. What are some of the "stupid," though well-meaning, things you have heard people say? Why are they "stupid"?

3. What sort of things have you heard people say that were interpretative in character? How do people often interpret another's sufferings? What sort of things do they say?

4. What is wrong with interpreting another's suffering? What does that presume? How is it like or unlike Job's friends?

5. In times of your grief, have there been any particularly helpful things people have said to you?

6. What comfort do you think Job imagines he could have provided his friends if they were in his situation? What would his lips have said? What did Job expect from his friends?

7. Why is reminding the sufferer about God better than interpreting the suffering? How is remembering (as Ps. 77:11-12; 143:5) better than explaining?

Consider this:

In this life there are very few relationships that engender a love so strong that we would die for that person. We occasionally hear of parents who have given their lives for their children, perhaps even a brother for a brother. On extremely rare occasions a friend for a friend. For whom would you die? Who would die for you? Meditate on the kind of unrelenting love required to bring this about before reading lesson 4.

4

ANCHOR ONE:
THE UNRELENTING LOVE OF GOD

In this lesson:

- ▶ God creates in order to share his unrelenting love in community with people
- ▶ We learn about God's unrelenting love through marriage and parenthood
- ▶ God's love for us was so great he allowed his Son to die for us

---

What, then, shall we say in response to this? If God is for us, who can be against us? He who did not spare his own Son, but gave him up for us all —how will he not also, along with him, graciously give us all things? Who will bring any charge against those whom God has chosen? It is God who justifies. Who is he that condemns? Christ Jesus, who died —more than that, who was raised to life —is at the right hand of God and is also interceding for us. Who shall separate us from the love of Christ? Shall trouble or hardship or persecution or famine or nakedness or danger or sword? As it is written:

"For your sake we face death all day long;
we are considered as sheep to be slaughtered."

No, in all these things we are more than conquerors through him who loved us. For I am convinced that neither death nor life, neither angels nor demons, neither the present nor the future, nor any powers, neither height nor depth, nor anything else in all creation, will be able to separate us from the love of God that is in Christ Jesus our Lord.

—Romans 8:31-39

The first anchor for the soul is the unrelenting love of God. This point seems so basic and so fundamental that it could almost go unstated. But that would be a mistake. The love of God is foundational for everything else we say about God. It defines his character and shapes his goal for us. It must be our starting point in thinking about God.

However, my anchor is not simply the "love of God," but it is the "unrelenting love of God." The word "unrelenting" is significant. It describes the nature of this love. It is a love that never quits. It is a love that never gives up. It is a love that overcomes every obstacle. It is a love that pursues us. God's love is no passive disposition, but is an active pursuit of humanity. God unrelentingly pursues us out of his great love.

CREATION

Creation was God's first act of unrelenting love. God created out of his overflowing love to include others in his loving communion. He created so he could share what he already possessed. The Father, Son, and Spirit in their eternal nature communed with each other in love (John 17:24), and they intended to share this love with others through creating a people in their image (John 17:26). God initiated creation for the sake of others so that they too might experience the wonder of blissful communion. The love of God is so great that he is willing to risk the bliss of his own communion so that others might participate in it.

When humanity rebelled and fell into its sinful habits, God's unrelenting love took the initiative to redeem. The biblical idea of election is focused in the thought that God took the initiative in redemption. Election means that God acted first. He decided that he would redeem us through Christ even before the foundation of the world. God elected us in Christ (Eph. 1:3-5). God made the first move. Our sin did not discourage his love, but his redemptive acts flow from that love.

What did God create? He created a community — a male and a female who would fill the earth with their descendants, and consequently fill the earth with God's glory (Gen. 1:28; 9:1). When God created Israel, he chose Abraham and Sarah whose descendants would be a people which would glorify God among the nations. When God created the church, he chose Christ who would be the author of salvation for the brothers and sisters he would bring to glory (Heb. 2:10). God has always intended a people for himself. Whether in the original act of creation or in the redemptive act of re-creation, God gathers a people for himself. God intends to share his love with a community.

> Whether in the original act of creation or in the redemptive act of re-creation, God gathers a people for himself.

This is a pervasive theme in Scripture. When God entered into covenant with Abraham, he promised him that he would not only be Abraham's God, but also the God of his descendants after him. Abraham's descendants would be God's people and he would be their God (Gen. 17:7-8). When God came to Israel in Egypt through Moses, he promised redemption and assured them that "I will take you as my own people, and I will be your God" (Exod. 6:7). When Israel set up the tabernacle in the wilderness, God's glory descended on it with the promise that there God would dwell among his people and be their God (Exod. 29:45; 40:34-35; Lev. 26:11-12). The glory was repeated with the completion of the temple under Solomon (1 Kgs. 8:11; 2 Chr. 5:14; 7:1-3). The prophets constantly reminded Israel of God's promise to be present among them (Ezek. 34:30). Israel would be God's people and he would be their God (Jer. 7:23; 11:4; 24:7; Ezek. 11:20; 14:11; 36:28; 37:27; Zech. 2:11; 8:8; 13:9).

Further, this promise was at the heart of the "new covenant." Through Jeremiah, God declared his intent to forgive Israel's sin so that he could fulfill his promise, that is, "I will be their God and they will be my people" (Jer. 31:33). Paul, in the context of thinking about the ministry of this new covenant (2 Cor. 3:6), reminds us that this promise has found expression in God's church where "we are the temple of the living God" (2 Cor. 6:16). Leviticus 26:11-12 is fulfilled in the church, as God has said: "I will live with them and walk among them, and I will be their God, and they will be my people" (2 Cor. 6:16 quoting Lev. 26:12). In the church God has a people for himself. But the ultimate goal of this promise is the dwelling of God in a

> The ultimate goal of God's promise is his dwelling with his people as a community in a new heaven and new earth.

new heaven and new earth with his people as a community that he will establish when the new age is consummated. When the new Jerusalem descends out of heaven, then a loud voice will announce: "Now the dwelling of God is with men, and he will live with them. They will be his people, and God himself will be with them and be their God" (Rev. 21:3).

This redemptive-historical motif, that God seeks a people for himself, demonstrates that God's intent in redemption/re-creation is to dwell with his people in a communion of love. God seeks fellowship with his people. Since re-creation is modeled after creation, God's original act of creation had the same intent. He created a community, a people, for himself. He created a people with whom he could share a communion of love. This goal shapes everything God does in history. It is because of this goal that God pursues humanity out of love. God's love means he will never give up his goal and he will pursue everyone for the sake of that goal.

HISTORY OF ISRAEL

Even though we wounded God's love, it could not be quenched. Even when Israel refused to know him, God would not give up on his people. The prophets often used the imagery of husband and wife to picture the relationship between God and Israel. Two texts are particularly

> Even though we wounded God's love, it could not be quenched.

striking. The first is Hosea 1–3. God told the prophet Hosea to love his adulterous wife Gomer "as the LORD loves the Israelites" (3:1). Hosea's re-marriage was a symbol of God's renewed love for unfaithful Israel. God suffered the pain of a broken promise. He suffered, like Hosea, the betrayal of an unfaithful wife. Nevertheless, so great is the love of God that he pledged that a day would come when Israel would no longer say "my master" but would say "my husband" (2:16). On that day God will show his love for his people, and declare "You are my people!" In turn, they will respond to him, "You are my God" (Hos. 2:23).

A second striking example of this metaphor is Ezekiel 16. God pledged himself to Israel in covenant and entered into a marriage relationship with her (16:8). He showered her with gifts, including costly garments, jewels, and exquisite food. Israel's fame spread among the nations because of the beauty the Lord had given her (16:9-14). But Israel "trusted in [her] beauty," and she became a prostitute (16:15). Even the children she bore to the Lord, she sacrificed on the altars to other gods with whom she prostituted herself (16:20-22). Because of her sins, God divorced her and in his "jealous anger" (16:38) he rained his wrath down upon her. Nevertheless, God declares his faithful love.

> God will renew his love on the ground of his own covenant and by his own atoning work.

"Yet I will remember the covenant I made with you in the days of your youth, and I will establish an everlasting covenant with you" (16:60). God will renew his love for her on the ground of his own covenant and by his own atoning work. God will act in love for his adulterous wife, and he will "make atonement" for her (16:63).

Another metaphor is the parent/child analogy, particularly as parents care for, weep over, and suffer with their children. The prophet Hosea (11:1-4) pictures God as a loving parent who redeemed his child from Egyptian bondage, taught him to walk, healed his broken spirit, and stooped to feed him. God loved Israel and treated them with wonderful kindnesses. He bound them with ties of love. God treated Israel like a mother eagle treats her young. He hovered over them and caught them when they fell. God "shielded [Israel] and cared for him, he guarded him as the apple of his eye" (Deut. 32:10-11). Yet, they rebelled and turned against him. As rebellious children, they spurned the love of their parent. Isaiah draws upon the same imagery. The Lord says, "I reared children and brought them up, but they have rebelled against me" (Isa. 1:2).

Nevertheless, the compassion of the Lord is great. "How can I give you up, Ephraim? How can I hand you over, Israel?" (Hos. 11:8). God will not treat them like any other nation. Rather, he declares, "My heart is changed within me; all my compassion is aroused" (11:8). God will not fully vent his wrath against his own child. Rather, God "will roar like a lion" and when he roars, "his children will come trembling from the west" (11:10). God will again settle them in their own homes (11:11). So also, in Isaiah, God is pictured as a mother who wishes to once again embrace her children, and as a determined mother, God will do so. "As a mother comforts her child," the Lord declares, "so will I comfort you" (Isa. 66:13).

God will not forget his people. He bore them and cared for them like a mother though he disciplined them like a father.

> In Isaiah, God is pictured as a mother who wishes to once again embrace her children

Despite their sin, God's people must not say, "The LORD has forsaken me, the Lord has forgotten me." God responds, "Can a mother forget the baby at her breast and have no compassion on the child she has borne? Though she may forget, I will not forget you" (Isa. 49:14-15). God will act to redeem because he suffers with his children. God suffers because of his children — as rebels they have broken his heart — but God also suffers with his children in his yearning to renew the fellowship that has been broken. God will not forget. Rather, God will redeem (Isa. 54:5-8).

God's love pursued Israel from the time he led them out of Egypt till the time he ransomed them from their exile. God's love meant that he would not give up on his people.

JESUS CHRIST

The climactic demonstration of this love is God's work in Jesus Christ. "While we were still sinners," Paul wrote, "Christ died for us" (Rom. 5:8). This is how we know that God is love, John wrote, because he "sent his Son as an atoning sacrifice for our sins" (1 John 4:10). The unrelenting love of God is expressed in the lengths to which God went to accomplish his goal of fellowship with us. God joined the human race, shared its weaknesses and its burdens, experienced its shame, and died on a cross. God sacrificed himself in Jesus Christ for the sake of others, and his love knew no limits. There was no cost that God would not pay for fellowship with his people, and he demonstrated this at the cross. God sacrificed all for the sake of his people. "He who did not spare his own Son, but gave him up for us all," Paul wrote, "how will he not also, along with him, graciously give us all things?" (Rom. 8:32).

> The unrelenting love of God is expressed in the lengths to which God went to accomplish his goal of fellowship with us.

God intends to have a people for himself with whom he can share his love. This is why he created, and it is why he redeems. This is why he unrelentingly pursues humanity, and this is why he became one of us and went to the cross. God has demonstrated his love.

When we look at the fallen world with all its pain and death, we can easily doubt that love. Where is God when evil surrounds us? Where is the love of God when my child dies? When we look within our fallen selves, we can easily doubt that God could ever love someone like me with all my faults. How can God love me when my own parents abuse me? How can God love me when even my own husband divorced me? How can God love me when I am so full of sin? The fallen world is filled with reasons for doubting God's love. But that is why God gave us his story.

The plot of the biblical story is the unceasing pursuit of God's love for a people who will return his love and share his communion. God is not looking for excuses to punish, nor is he looking for opportunities to show off his wrath. God yearns for his people, pursues them with compassion, and humbles himself in costly self-sacrifice for the sake of his people. God is not seeking an excuse to punish, but an opportunity to share. God is not seeking a pretext for his wrath, but an occasion for fellowship.

> The plot of the biblical story is the unceasing pursuit of God's love for a people who will return his love and share his communion.

CONCLUSION

When the doubts creep in and the fears debilitate, I remember the cross of Jesus Christ. I can stand beside the coffin of my wife and doubt God's love, but I cannot kneel at the foot of the cross and doubt it. God has offered me an indubitable testimony of his love. Despite all the contrary witnesses that fill a fallen world, God entered history and demonstrated his love for us in the incarnation, ministry, death, and resurrection of Jesus Christ. Nothing — neither death nor demons nor hunger nor hardship nor poverty — can separate us from that love. God's love pursues us in such a way that he will never quit, and he will do whatever it takes (as he did in Jesus) to commune with his people.

Reflecting on Lesson Four

1. Do you consciously or unconsciously tell yourself that God's love for you is conditional, limited, or dependent upon your performance? What does it mean to say that "God's love will never quit"? What practical difference does that make?

2. Thinking about Psalm 136, what lines of praise would you add from your own life that reflect God's faithful love to you? Where in your experience has God demonstrated faithful love?

3. What is the greatest demonstration of God's faithful love? How does God in Jesus reveal a love that never quits? What examples from the life, ministry, and death of Jesus can you remember that reveal his love?

4. If God has demonstrated faithful love to us, how do we demonstrate faithful love to each other? How do we perfect the love of God in our hearts by loving the brothers? What does that look like practically? Give an example from your own experience.

Consider this:

Imagine this scenario: Your eleven-year-old daughter has been invited to her best friend's birthday party. She has been looking forward to it for weeks because they will be going to the local theme park. However, your mother, who lives at some distance from you, has just been told she has only a few weeks to live. It is difficult for you to get away, so this may be the only weekend for you to see her and for her to see her children and grandchildren before she dies. You know your child will be heartbroken to miss the party, but there are no other options. How would you expect your child to react? Will she be angry? Will she lash out at you? Will she tell you how unfair it is (more upset that she must miss the party than that her grandmother is dying)? How will you react to her? Will you be harsh and hard? Or will you be understanding and hurt with her? Now read lesson 5 about how we cry out when life is unfair and how God reacts to our hurts.

5

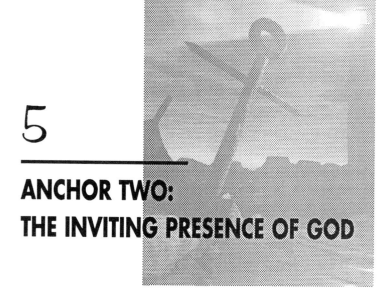

ANCHOR TWO:
THE INVITING PRESENCE OF GOD

In this lesson:

- ▶ Being honest with our emotions before God
- ▶ God wants to hear our laments
- ▶ Turning lamentation into praise

I cry aloud to God,
aloud to God, that he may hear me.
In the day of my trouble I seek the Lord;
in the night my hand is stretched out without wearying;
my soul refuses to be comforted.
I think of God, and I moan;
I meditate, and my spirit faints.   Selah.

You keep my eyelids from closing;
I am so troubled that I cannot speak.
I consider the days of old,
and remember the years of long ago.
I commune with my heart in the night;
I meditate and search my spirit:
Will the Lord spurn forever,
and never again be favorable?
Has his steadfast love ceased forever?
Are his promises at an end for all time?
Has God forgotten to be gracious?
Has he in anger shut up his compassion?
—Psalm 77:1-9, NRSV

The second anchor for the soul is the inviting presence of God. There are times when we feel abandoned by God. There are times when we feel, like the author of Psalm 77, that the promises of God have failed and that the love of God has ceased. What do faithful believers do in those times? Do we keep silent and hide our disappointment with God? Or, do we speak to God honestly about our feelings?

God, I believe, invites us to speak to him honestly. He invites us to share the burdens of our heart with him. The psalmists pled for this kind of honesty with God. "Cast your cares on the LORD and he will sustain you" (Ps. 55:22). Or, "Trust in him at all times, O people; pour out your hearts to him, for God is our refuge" (Ps. 62:8). The Psalms model this kind of honesty with God. "Hear me, O God, as I voice my complaint" (Ps. 64:1). Or, "I pour out my complaint before him; before him I tell my trouble" (Ps. 142:2).

God invites us to speak, and he promises us that he will be near. He will listen and he will comfort. God will come to us in our lament, hear our cry, and comfort us in our troubles.

PSALMS OF LAMENT

When fallenness invades our lives, when pain, disease, or death strikes our loved ones, our hearts cry out in protest. We sense that something is terribly wrong with the world. We sense that this is not the way things are supposed to be. Indeed, it is not the way God created the world. God created peace, life, harmony, and joy in the Garden, but sin has decimated that world. It has broken the original harmony. Death has entered God's good creation. Our protests, then, are yearnings for the original harmony. They are a natural response to the fallenness we now experience. We protest against death and we refuse to accept its appropriateness in God's creation.

The laments of Scripture are filled with those kinds of protests. The people of God cry out to their God under the burden of fallenness. The Psalms provide example after example of faithful lament. The people of God confront their God in anger, bitterness, doubt, confusion, and bewilderment. They ask God, "Why?" (Ps. 10:1; 22:1; 42:9; 43:2; 44:23-24; 74:1,11; 79:10; 80:12; 88:14) and "How long?" (Ps. 6:3; 13:1-2; 35:16-17; 74:10-11; 79:5; 80:4; 89:46; 90:13; 94:3; 119:84). They ask God, "Where are you?" and "Why have you hidden yourself from your people?" (Ps. 13:1; 30:7; 44:24; 69:17; 88:14; 89:46; 102:2; 143:7). They ask God, "When will you bring justice to the earth?" (Ps. 58). They complain, question, and weep. The story of God is filled with the protests of his people because his people have nowhere else to turn.

> The story of God is filled with the protests of his people because his people have nowhere else to turn.

Psalm 13 is a typical lament that moves from complaint (vv. 1-2) to petition (vv. 3-4) and then to praise (vv. 5-6). It beautifully illustrates the typical structure of lament psalms. The psalmist prayed:

> How long, O LORD? Will you forget me forever?
>> How long will you hide your face from me?
> How long must I wrestle with my thoughts
>> and every day have sorrow in my heart?
>> How long will my enemy triumph over me?
> Look on me and answer, O LORD my God.
>> Give light to my eyes, or I will sleep in death;
> my enemy will say, "I have overcome him,"
>> and my foes will rejoice when I fall.
> But I trust in your unfailing love;
>> my heart rejoices in your salvation.
> I will sing to the LORD,
>> for he has been good to me.

Psalm 13 asks God four questions, each of which begins with "How long?" The first two questions address God's involvement. How long will God continue to "forget" his servant and "hide" his face from him? The psalmist understands that God controls his universe, and he attributes his present circumstances to God's action or inaction. There must be a real answer. The psalmist assumes that God is responsible for the circumstances of his suffering and so he addresses him. The second two questions address the fallen circumstance in which the psalmist finds himself. In particular, he asks how long sorrow and pain must fill his heart while his enemies triumph over him. The questions are a complaint about God's inaction and the psalmist's sorrow. Where is God? What is he doing? Why does he not act?

Psalm 13 does not reveal the psalmist's particular problem. It speaks in generalities though it was occasioned by some painful event. However, as it appears, it speaks to all disorientation. It speaks honestly and boldly to God about the fallenness of the world. It is an honest appraisal that something is not right with the world. Lament functions to bring the fallenness of the world into the throne room of God and to question God about it. It is the means by which God's people bring real questions about real pain into the real presence of God.

Lament functions to bring the fallenness of the world into the throne room of God and to question God about it.

Psalm 13 also petitions God to act. Three times the psalmist invokes the name of God and the covenant relationship that exists between them. He uses the name of God, Yahweh, twice (13:1,3) and affirms that Yahweh is his God ("my God," 13:3). He then offers three petitions: "look on me," "answer," and "give light to my eyes." These redemptive petitions call for God to notice his suffering servant, to answer his pleas, and to redeem him from the darkness. The psalmist may fear that his death is near which would delight his enemies (13:3-4). The petitioner wants redemption. There is also an implied imprecation. God must not permit his enemies to rejoice over the demise of God's servant. The honor of God is at stake if one of God's people dies. The petition arises not only out of the human need of the moment but also out of a zeal for God's holy name.

Given the current make up of our hymnals, it surprises most people to discover that almost half of Psalms is lament. The emphasis in modern worship falls heavily upon songs of confidence, praise, thanksgiving, and joy. Little appears in our hymnals that is genuinely lament, except for some penitential or confessional hymns. Modern Christians are uncomfortable with lament. It is too bold, too daring, and involves God too intimately with his world. It is a cry to God about suffering, and modern Christians want to keep God at a distance from suffering. God must not get his hands dirty. Yet, approximately half of the psalms are laments and the largest single grouping of psalms is individual lament. When fallenness breaks into the lives of God's people, they call upon their God. They

> Modern Christians want to keep God at a distance from suffering.

invoke God's faithfulness, steadfast love, and sovereignty in order to complain, petition his action, and ultimately praise him.

GOD AS PATIENT LISTENER

Yet those laments are in Scripture precisely because God invites us to lament. He invites us into his presence to speak our hearts to him. God seeks communion — real communion. He does not want ritual repetitions or high-sounding platitudes. He wants to hear the hearts of his people. He wants his people to share their hearts with him. God wants to engage them in genuine communion. But there is no authentic communion when God's people are not honest with their God. Can we deceive God by "putting on a good face" in prayer while our heart is breaking? God does not seek such superficiality. Rather, he yearns to hear the cries of his people so he can respond to their hurts and share their burden.

God invites us to speak our protests and to voice our laments. God is not offended by such protestations. He is patient. He understands lament because he himself has experienced it. God lamented the sinfulness and destruction of Israel through the weeping prophet Jeremiah (Jer. 8:21–9:2). Jesus lamented the stubbornness of Israel as he wept over Jerusalem (Matt. 23:37).

Indeed, Jesus voiced his lament on the cross in the words of the psalmist, "My God, My God, why have you forsaken me?" (Ps. 22:1; Matt. 26:46). God himself in Jesus Christ has lamented. God understands the pain and alienation that gives rise to lament, and he understands how faith must complain because the world does not look like faith expects.

> He understands lament because he himself has experienced it.

Even now, God listens to the questions of the saints gathered around his throne. Even in the throne room of God the saints of God continue to question him, saying, "How long, Sovereign Lord, holy and true, until you judge the inhabitants of the earth and avenge our blood?" (Rev. 6:10).

God is a loving father who listens to his children. He does not listen to scold, but to heal. He does not respond in anger to these protests. Rather, he responds in love. These protests do not repulse God. On the contrary, they evoke God's loving presence. Like a parent who comforts a hurting child, so God wraps his arms around the protesting believer. God absorbs the pain of these protests and his love overwhelms them. God's presence invades our laments to comfort and reassure us of his love. This is why the laments in Psalms end in praise. The people of God sense God's presence, his comfort, and his faithfulness. God listens and he responds. God offers his "sanctuary" presence to lamenters.

THE COMFORTING PRESENCE OF GOD

Psalm 13 illustrates this classic move in lament psalms from complaint and petition to praise and thanksgiving. At some point in most lament psalms (44 and 88 are two exceptions), there comes a moment where the writer shifts from complaint to praise. This transition is signaled in English by the word "but." Psalm 13 moves from complaint to petition, and then introduces praise by declaring, "But I trust in your unfailing love" (13:5). The psalm of lament, then, ends in praise. It ends with confidence and trust. It rejoices in the God who provides salvation and deliverance. What occasioned this mood swing? Why does the tone of the psalm change from lament to praise?

Some have argued that we need to envision an "oracle of salvation" which offers a response to the lament. In other words, the psalmist offers his complaint and petition as in 13:1-4, and then waits for a divine response. Once he receives this response, he then writes 13:5-6. This may have been enacted within the liturgy of the temple worship where a spokesperson for God would respond to the lament and the worshiper would then offer his vow of praise or affirm his trust in God. There can be little doubt that this sometimes happened. Indeed, we find both Job (42:1-6) and Habakkuk (3:1ff) responding to divine theophanies or oracles. They offered their laments and then in response to the divine theophanies they humbled themselves before God and expressed their ultimate trust in his purposes. There are also examples in the writings of the prophets (cf. Isa. 59:3ff; Joel 2:1ff; Jer. 51:36ff). It is possible that this is what is envisioned here.

However, some psalms may be translated with a "nevertheless" rather than a "but." Instead of hearing a word from God that engenders this praise, the vow of praise may arise out of the confidence of faith. Despite the dire circumstances of the lament, the petitioner through prayer experiences the reassuring presence of God. The change is not just a change in mood but is the experience of God's presence which moves the heart from lament to praise. It is a sanctuary experience — an experience of God's presence which gives rise to praise.

Confidence in God's steadfast love moves the petitioners to praise God when just moments ago they were complaining to him. But the complaints and the praise arise out of the same attitude — faith in God's loving presence. They complain to God because they believe, and they learn to praise God through their lament. Through prayer and lamentation petitioners move to a new understanding of faith, a deeper appreciation of God's grace, and the assurance of God's presence. God has already begun to act. He is present to comfort his people, and he will ultimately vindicate them. "My comfort in my suffering is this," the psalmist writes, "your promise preserves my life" (119:50). Even though he asks in lament, "When will you comfort me?" (119:82), he knows his comfort is found in God's steadfast love (119:76; cf. Lam. 3:19-26). Prayer as lamentation moves the people of God to a deeper understanding and a relational experience of that love. God offers his people a "sanctuary" experience in the midst of lament.

Prayer does not simply function as a vehicle for venting. It is the cry of faith. It hopes for a sympathetic ear and a resolution to the despair of lament. However, like Job, we do not always get the answer we seek, but we often receive the answer we need. What Job wanted was an explanation, and what he got was the comforting, reassuring presence of God. Our laments ask real questions and God offers himself in communion, and by the power of the Holy Spirit he creates hope, comfort, and peace in the midst of our lament (Rom. 15:13).

CONCLUSION

The psalmists approach God with questions, despair, and lament. They ask God "why?" and "how long?" They seek his face. They seek his communion. They desire God's presence and his deliverance. But they ask their God questions.

The continuity here is that the people of God have always approached God boldly with their questions because they know he is the Sovereign Lord who can redeem. Prayer moves us into the presence of God where we are awed by his wisdom, power, and love. God is present to us through prayer, through lament, through worship. In worship, in a sanctuary experience, we find God's strength by which our faith is empowered to live through the lament and ultimately to break out in praise. God acts to comfort his people through their laments. God provides "songs in the night" as we engage him in prayer. God invites us to lament, and he responds in grace.

When fallenness cripples my life, I go to God in protest. My faith laments the brokenness of the world and cries out for God's deliverance. It yearns for the inbreaking of God's full reign in the world. As I watch my son slowly deteriorate and I foresee his eventual death, I protest and I pray for the fullness of God's kingdom now. I yearn for the day when death will no longer have dominion over my son. My laments protest death. They protest fallenness. And God hears my prayer and shares his comforting presence with me as I wait for the fullness of God's victory.

Reflecting on Lesson Five

1. Do you have an experience you can share where you expressed anger, disappointment, or frustration with God? Why did you feel this way about God and what did you tell him?

2. Why do we feel that honest prayers of doubt and disappointment are misguided? Why do we feel guilty when we pray such prayers? Should we?

Why or why not? How does confidence in God's steadfast love help us pray these prayers?

3. How do the lament Psalms help us deal with this guilt? How are they models for our own lament? The next time you are traumatized by illness, will you be able to pray Psalm 6 without feeling guilty? Will you have the confidence to pray Psalm 13?

4. What in your life makes you cry, "How long? O Lord, How Long?" Have you prayed about it honestly or have you put on a "smiley face" for God? Don't you think honesty would make a difference? What kind of difference would it make?

Consider this:

Think of one or more circumstances of life which you have known about and watched from the outside and then experienced firsthand. For example, most of us know about marriage through our parents and friends and even books, but eventually the majority of us will experience it for ourselves. Write down as many ways as you can the difference between knowing about this (these) experience(s) and actually participating in it (them).

6

ANCHOR THREE:
THE CARING EMPATHY OF GOD

In this lesson:

▶ God's own experiences with pain, betrayal, and rejection

▶ The nearness of God as he shares with us when we are in pain

▶ In the incarnation God added human experience to his understanding of grief and suffering

---

Since the children have flesh and blood, he too shared in their humanity so that by his death he might destroy him who holds the power of death – that is, the devil – and free those who all their lives were held in slavery by their fear of death. For surely it is not angels he helps, but Abraham's descendants. For this reason he had to be made like his brothers in every way, in order that he might become a merciful and faithful high priest in service to

God, and that he might make atonement for the sins of the people. Because he himself suffered when he was tempted, he is able to help those who are being tempted.

—Hebrews 2:14-18

The third anchor for the soul is the caring empathy of God. Often believers sense that God is rather distant to their cares and concerns. Some believe that God does not understand the depth of hurt and pain because he resides in some kind of eternal bliss that is unaffected by the suffering of this world. How can God understand the pain of a rebellious child or spousal betrayal? How can God know what it is like to feel the struggle of temptation?

But God is not an outsider when it comes to suffering. God himself has suffered. He understands suffering because he has experienced suffering. God understands. God knows what it is like to be rejected by a spouse or spurned by a rebellious child. God was rejected and betrayed by Israel. God knows what it is like to be tempted (Heb. 4:15) and knows what it is like to hunger and thirst. God in Jesus Christ was tempted and experienced the weaknesses of our flesh. God understands. God empathizes with his people in their fallenness.

THE SYMPATHY OF GOD

We have all sympathized with others who have experienced the world's fallenness. We have all sat in funeral homes with friends or written the occasional sympathy card. We sympathize with people when we hurt because they hurt and we weep because they weep. God himself feels this sympathy. Our God is the weeping God who grieves over sin, pain, and death. God is no stoic statue who is impervious to our hurts. God does not sit enthroned in an undisturbed joyful bliss. On the contrary, God weeps over our fallenness. He mourns over his corrupted creation. He grieves over the loss of fellowship with his people.

God has suffered ever since his people chose their own way and fell into sin. God grieves the loss of his people. Ever since the grief of God asked, "Who told you that you were naked?" (Gen. 3:11), God's heart has been heavy. Yet, God showed his mercy to Adam and Eve by renewing life among them with a child (Gen. 4:1-2). It reached a boiling point in Genesis 6 when God saw how wicked humanity had become and

> God has suffered ever since his people chose their own way and fell into sin.

he "was grieved that he had made man on the earth, and his heart was filled with pain" (6:6). Yet God showed his mercy in Noah (Gen. 6:8-9). God was grieved in the wilderness when his people rebelled against him and put him to the test (Ps. 78:40-41). Yet God showed his mercy by ultimately bringing his people through the wilderness and into the promised land (Ps. 78:54-55). Humanity's sin is God's sorrow, and when we rebel or forsake his love, God's Spirit is grieved (Isa. 63:10; Eph. 4:30).

God suffers when his people seek their own path instead of finding joy in his loving fellowship, and God truly rejoices when his people return to that fellowship. God has a heart. He hurts when fellowship is broken and is enriched when fellowship is restored. While God is devoid of uncontrolled passions, God is nevertheless filled with the emotions of love, jealousy, compassion, mercy, patience, and anger. God is emotionally involved with his creation so that he shares their sorrows and their joys. God is not impassible. God is moved and stirred by the course of human history. While God cannot be manipulated or controlled by some outside power, God responds, relates, and reacts to the tragedies and victories of human existence. The weeping prophet speaks for the weeping God (Jer. 8:21–9:3; 9:8-10; 12:7-12; 15:5-9).

THE EMPATHY OF GOD

But God is more than sympathetic. He is also empathetic. God does not stand off at a distance and merely pity his fallen creation. He does more. He comes near and enters into our experience and actually shares the fallenness of the world with us. God not only weeps over my hurt, but he shares the experience of my hurt with me. God not only weeps over the eventual death of my son, he himself has experienced the death of his own Son. God not only weeps over the rebellion of a runaway child, but God himself knows the pain that rebellious children create in the hearts of their parents. God himself has experienced the pain and hurt of the fallen world. He understands. He not only sympathizes, he also empathizes with us.

> God not only weeps over my hurt, but he shares the experience of my hurt with me.

God suffers in the same way that a betrayed spouse or a heartbroken parent suffers. God understands the hurt of betrayal and he understands the hurt of a rebellious child. God yearns for his people as a mother yearns for her children. God empathizes with hurt spouses and abandoned parents.

God is willing to humble himself for the sake of his people. Because he loves, he is willing to receive back an adulterous wife. Because he loves, he will embrace a returning prodigal. The God who sits above the heavens will descend to earth in order to help his people, demonstrate his love, and seek a people for himself. This is the "incarnational" character of God. The one "who sits enthroned on high" also "stoops down to look on the heavens and the earth." He will raise up the poor and the needy and seat them "with princes," and he will settle "the barren woman in her home as a happy mother of children" (Ps. 113:5-9). The Sovereign God humbles himself to care for the poor and needy. "Though the LORD is on high, he looks upon the lowly" (Ps. 138:6).

THE EMPATHETIC INCARNATION OF GOD

The nature of divine experience is different from human experience. God sympathizes with us. He feels our pain through his own loving nature. He hurts with us. He knows what we know, but has not experienced what we have experienced except in the Incarnate One. The divine experience does not involve hunger, thirst, or temptation. The divine experience does not have a human experiential content.

> In the incarnation God actually experiences what his divine nature cannot.

The incarnation is the human experience of God. In the incarnation God actually experiences what his divine nature cannot: hunger, thirst, temptation, and death. In the incarnation the divine one becomes a fully empathetic God rather than simply the sympathetic God.

The empathetic character of God fully revealed itself in the incarnation, life, and ministry of Jesus Christ. The Son did not "exploit" his equality with the Father (Phil. 2:6, NRSV), but humbled himself. The one who existed from eternity in the form of

God took on the form of a servant (Phil. 2:7). Though the Son is the one "through whom all things came" (1 Cor. 8:6), he became a creature. Though he was Son, yet he learned obedience by the things which he suffered (Heb. 5:8). He was "rich," but he became "poor" (2 Cor. 8:9). The Word, the instrument of creation, became flesh and dwelt among us. The one who from the beginning was with the Father came into the world as one of us (John 1:1-3,14-18).

God in Jesus Christ humbled himself. As one who became human, he shared the fullness of our fallenness. The Son was tempted. He hungered, thirsted, experienced pain, and ultimately died. The humiliation of God in Christ was his identification with us in our fallenness. From his birth to baptism to death — he stood with the lowly. He stood with sinners. He was born among shepherds, baptized with those who confessed sin, and died between transgressors. Without the guilt of sin and without ever sinning himself, he shared our fallenness. He suffered the curse which Adamic sin brought upon the world. He experienced the world's fallenness through its pain, tears, and death.

As noted above, there is a sense in which God is empathetic in the Old Testament. God hurts with his people. He knows the pain of a rebellious child. He knows the pain of losing someone in death. God shares the experience of grief with his world. However, the

> On the cross God shared our experience of death rather than merely sympathizing with that experience at a distance.

incarnation renders God empathetic with us in a unique way. On the cross God shared our experience of death rather than merely sympathizing with that experience at a distance. God as human being participates in death itself. In the incarnation, God and human beings have the same experience. God identifies with us. In his incarnation, he takes upon himself the suffering of the world's ills. God bears the brunt of evil by subjecting himself to its cruelty and horror. God himself enters fallenness and experiences it. By so doing, he reveals, as he could in no other way, the reality, depth and costly nature of his forgiving love. Divine love and forgiveness are shown most clearly in the lengths to which our God is prepared to go to win the love of the loveless. God did not send a representative, but he came personally. God actually bore the suffering rather than simply sending his condolences. God not only sent a sympathy card, but he joined in the suffering empathetically.

The events in Jesus' life give meaning to this empathy. While his whole life and ministry involve him in the human experience, there are three historic symbols of this identification: (a) his birth where he took on human flesh, (b) his baptism where he identified with sinners, and (c) his cross where he identified with our fallen suffering, pain, and shame. In each case, God participates in human fallenness and experiences the suffering associated with each. In each case, God humbles himself to identify with sinners. In his birth, God joined the human race in the context of a fallen world. God came in the flesh so that he could experience authentic suffering along with his people. God's flesh was no sham but a genuine participation in human reality. Jesus submitted to a baptismal ritual designed for penitent believers who had confessed their sins. It was a baptism of repentance for the remission of sins (Luke 3:3; Mark 1:5). Jesus, then, identified with sinners through his own baptism, just as he also identified with them in his death (Luke 22:37; 23:32-33). He was crucified in weakness between two thieves. God became weak for our sakes

(2 Cor. 13:4) and the one who knew no sin became sin for us (2 Cor. 5:21). He suffered the curse for us (Gal. 3:13).

Through sharing this suffering, Jesus, the Son of God, is able to empathize and understand human weakness. He can understand it because he has personally experienced it. He empathizes with our weaknesses because he has shared our fallen life. He is able to intercede for us and help us because he himself was tempted (Heb. 2:18), and he is an empathetic high priest because he has experienced human weakness himself though without sin (Heb. 4:15). Jesus, the Son of God, was so fully immersed in human experience that he was tempted in every way that we are, yet without sin.

God suffered with us in Jesus Christ. He lamented with us in his own suffering. He himself voiced lament as he hung on the cross (Matt. 27:46 quoting Ps. 22:1). But it is only in our own suffering that we learn that God suffers. It is only in our own risking that we learn the depth of God's risk-

> It is only when we behold the cross that we see the tear-filled eyes of God.

taking love. It is only when we behold the cross that we see the tear-filled eyes of God. God is not only the God of the sufferers but the God who suffers, and who suffers with sufferers.

In Jesus, God experienced fallenness. He experienced pain, fatigue, thirst, hunger, grief, and death. In Jesus, God wept at the tomb of a friend (John 11:35). In Jesus, God experienced the humiliating shame of the cross. In Jesus, God shared our weaknesses with us, experienced our temptations and trials, and endured our shame. God came near in Jesus to sit on the mourner's bench with us. He understands the pain. He has experienced it in the flesh. God experienced my humanity and my pain in Jesus Christ.

CONCLUSION

God, then, is no mere distant relative who only hears about our hurts and sends a sympathy card. God does not stand off in a corner to watch us grieve or to pity us at a distance. On the contrary, God joined us in our humanity to share our grief, to experience our fallenness, and to empathize with our pain. In Jesus, God himself shares our laments over fallenness. God truly understands because he truly became one of us in Jesus Christ. Consequently, Jesus is able "to help those who are being tempted" because "he himself suffered when he was tempted" (Heb. 2:18).

Our hurts, pains, cries, and cares are *his*. He knows them. He has felt them. He has prayed them. God sits with us in the funeral home because he himself has experienced the fallenness of death. He can grieve with us while sitting beside us as God himself expresses his own grief over the fallenness of the world. God empathizes with his fallen creation and understands its hurt.

When fallenness surrounds me and I again feel its pain, I remember that God himself has also experienced that same hurt. He knows. He understands. He has been there, and so he is now here for me. He sits with me, weeps with me, and yearns for the new age just as I do.

Reflecting on Lesson Six

1. What is the difference between sympathy and empathy?

2. In what ways is God sympathetic with his creation?

3. In what ways is the God of Israel empathetic with his creation?

4. How is God empathetic in Jesus Christ? What does the incarnation mean for God's understanding of human fallenness and weakness?

5. What is the motive of God's empathy? Why did God express his empathy in the incarnation? Why did he go this far?

6. What does God's empathy say about the depth of his love? Would you join another in their suffering just to share it?

7. What is the comfort that God offers through this empathy? How does the fact that "God understands" affect your experience of suffering?

8. How do we model God's empathy in comforting sufferers? How does this affect our understanding of what "comforting" is?

Consider this:

Most of the world wrestles with some form of this question: If God is good and God is sovereign, why does he allow (violence, pain, anger, hatred, natural disasters, loss; fill in the blank)? Write out some of the thoughts you have had on this question and some of the possible answers you may have come up with. How do your thoughts fit with a good God? With a sovereign God?

7

ANCHOR FOUR:
THE UNLIMITED SOVEREIGNTY OF GOD

In this lesson:

▶ God's sovereignty includes power over the troubles that befall us
▶ God's ultimate goal is not our sensual happiness but communion with him
▶ Trusting God is rooted in the confidence that whatever he allows in our lives is because he is faithful to his ultimate goal

---

I know that the Lord is great,
that our Lord is greater than all gods.
The Lord does whatever pleases him,
in the heavens and on the earth,
in the seas and all their depths.

—Psalm 135:5-6

And we know that in all things God works for the good of those who love him, who have been called according to his purpose.

—Romans 8:28

The fourth anchor for the soul is the unlimited sovereignty of God. This is the most problematic of the five anchors to grasp and understand. It is the hardest to trust. It is difficult because the world seems so chaotic, and it is difficult because the work of God's sovereignty is so mysterious.

There are many theories of providence available on the contemporary scene. They each interpret sovereignty differently. Such diversity creates confusion and many despair over drawing any confidence from the assertion of God's sovereignty because there are so many disagreements about its nature. How can the believer find an anchor here?

Despite the diversity, I believe there are some sure moorings to this anchor that offer a sufferer confidence. Whatever theory of providence one may hold, I think there is sufficient common ground for fellow-sufferers who believe the biblical story of God to draw strength and assurance from God's sovereign work in the world.

THE ENTHRONED GOD

Fallenness often makes us wonder whether God really is in control of his world. Perhaps God does care, but he cannot do anything about it. Perhaps God loves us, but he cannot help. The biblical story, however, does not picture God this way. Even when it appears that Satan and his cohorts have the upper hand, as when the Roman empire persecuted God's saints, God still sits on his throne (Revelation 4). God is still in control. Indeed, God controls the extent and length of the persecution (Rev. 6:9-10). Satan cannot dethrone God. Fallenness does not undermine God's sovereignty. God still sits on his throne. God remains in control even when my circumstances are difficult.

The Psalms are filled with the confidence that God is King even though everything is not what it is supposed to be. Indeed, the confidence of the psalmists, even in their laments, is that God is so sovereign over the world that he is able to deliver, save, and rescue.

> God remains in control even when my circumstances are difficult.

God can deliver his saints out of trouble because he is the Sovereign Lord. The Lord God reigns (Ps. 93:1; 96:10; 97:1; 98:6; 99:1; 146:10).

For example, Psalm 10 is a lament song that begins by questioning God. The psalmist asks, "Why, O LORD, do you stand far off? Why do you hide yourself in times of trouble?" (10:1). The believer is surrounded by evil. The wicked oppress and afflict the weak and poor, and the arrogant boast about their prosperity. He creates trouble for God's people, and he assures himself that God does not notice his evil (10:2-11). But the psalmist cries for God to do something. "Arise, LORD! Lift up your hand, O God. Do not forget the helpless" (10:12). This petition is rooted in two anchors: (1) God cares, and (2) God reigns. God notices his afflicted people, and he will act on their behalf. The psalmist prays, "But you, O God, do see trouble and grief; you consider it to take it in hand" (10:14). God hears the prayers of his people, and he will respond to their afflictions (10:17-18). God is able because he is the sovereign King. "The LORD is King for ever and ever" (10:16). God can break the arm of the wicked because he is the sovereign Lord. God can rescue the oppressed because he is King.

Trouble does not dethrone God. On the contrary, God reigns over trouble. God can protect his people from trouble (Psalms 17, 91). God controls the nations around Israel so that they do not afflict his people except as he permits (Psalm 9). God judges humanity and decides whom he will exalt and whom he will bring down (Psalm 75). God conquers sickness and heals diseases (Psalms 30, 116), and he rescues his people from their enemies (Psalms 18, 69). "The righteous cry out, and the LORD hears them; he delivers them from all their troubles. . . . A righteous man may have many troubles, but the LORD delivers him from them all" (Ps. 34:17,19).

No one experienced more trouble than Job. But God is the one who initiated Job's trouble by calling Satan's attention to him. Satan is aware of Job. He does not deny Job's external righteousness, but he does attack his integrity. "Sure," Satan says, "Job is righteous. Why shouldn't he be? You have protected him from every disaster and given him every blessing. Who wouldn't serve you under those circumstances?" According to Satan, Job is righteous for a different reason than God will admit. Job serves God for profit. Satan accuses Job of selfishness. Job's worship is self-centered and self-interested. It is a "fair-weather" faith. God has bribed Job. Consequently, Satan asks, "Does Job fear God for nothing?" (Job 1:9).

> Satan's implied accusation is an accusation against all believers.

Satan's implied accusation is an accusation against all believers. It says that we serve and love God for the rewards. Satan asserts that the basis of faith is profit or personal gain. As long as believers are prosperous, healthy, and happy, they will serve God. But let God permit some trouble, permit the loss of a family member or the loss of a job, then believers will lose hope in him and reject him. Faith only exists when it is profitable. Believers are only faithful when they are happy. Job himself acknowledges that this is the attitude of the wicked. They ask, "Who is the Almighty, that we should serve him? What would we gain by praying to him?" (Job 21:15). Will anyone love God even when there is nothing to be gained other than God's fellowship? Will anyone love God just to enjoy his fellowship? Will Job worship God despite the fact that he has lost everything? This is the trial of Job, and the test of all genuine faith. Job, however, will not give up his faith nor curse God despite his sufferings. Job rejects the counsel of the wicked. He knows "their prosperity is not in their own hands, so [he] stand[s] aloof from the counsel of the wicked" (Job 21:16).

Satan recognizes that he cannot act against Job under the present circumstances. God had put a "hedge" or fence around him to protect him from disasters (Job 1:10). God had limited Satan's access to Job. Satan understands that if Job is to be tested, if disaster is to come upon him, then God must act. God must remove his protection. Thus, he challenges God, "But stretch out your hand and strike everything he has, and he will surely curse you to your face" (Job 1:11).

The hand of God, a metaphor for the power or activity of God, must move against Job if disaster is to strike his family. God must lift his hand — extend his power, act in some manner — if the heavenly council is to discover whether Job serves God for profit. Indeed, when Job passes the first test, God complains to Satan that "you incited me against him to ruin him without any reason" (Job 2:3). God recognizes his responsibility for the test. Again, in the second trial, Satan challenges God to "stretch out [his] hand and strike his flesh and bones" (Job 2:4). An act of God is required if Job is to experience calamity. The power went from God's hand to Satan's hand (Job 1:11-12; 2:5-6). It was God's power, in the hands of Satan, that tested Job. Satan wielded God's power by God's own permission.

At the very least we must say that God permitted Satan to afflict Job when he could have prevented it. In fact, God had previously prevented Satan. But God lifted the hedge, and placed the power to act into Satan's hands with restrictions (Job 1:12; 2:6). In the first test, Satan could not touch the person of Job, but he could destroy his property, servants, and family. In the second test, Satan could not kill Job, but he could inflict severe pain upon his body. Nevertheless, God was responsible even though Satan may have been the direct agent. He was at least responsible in the sense that he gave Satan *permission* and *power.* God could have refused Satan's challenge. He could have restricted Satan further than he did. He could have said, "Satan, you can destroy his property, but not his children." God determined the kind of power he would put into the hand of Satan, and he

> God determined the kind of power he would put into the hand of Satan, and he determined its limitations.

determined its limitations. God bears the ultimate responsibility for the trouble that came upon Job because it did not have to come at all. God could have kept the "hedge" in place, or he could have prevented what Satan sought to implement. God's hand acted against Job. God sovereignly decided to test Job in response to Satan's accusation.

God controlled the trouble that overwhelmed Job. He permitted its implementation, and he could have stopped it at any time. Indeed, eventually, he does stop it (Job 42:10-11). Satan was not a loose cannon, but God sovereignly reigned over his activities. Trouble began for Job only when God decided to permit it, and the trouble ended only when God decided to end it. God reigns over trouble.

GOD'S GOAL FOR HIS PEOPLE

Because God loves, because God listens, and because God empathizes, we trust that God has the best interests of his people in mind. God has a purpose for the trials and troubles his people experience. God cares and God is sovereign. Nothing on God's part, then, is malicious and nothing is arbitrary. God is praised for his "love and faithfulness" and also for his sovereignty, "Our God is in heaven; he does whatever pleases him" (Ps. 115:1,3). God intends to bless his people out of his love and to secure those blessings by his sovereignty. God has a goal for his people and everything that happens serves that goal.

> God's goal is to establish and enjoy an eternal communion with us.

But that goal is not necessarily our earthly happiness, but our heavenly fellowship with him. God is more interested in our faith than our pleasure. God's goal is to establish and enjoy an eternal communion with us. God is more interested in our holy communion with him than whether we are healthy or wealthy. Whether or not God permits or causes any particular event in the world, it is enough to say that God is sovereign over all events, and that nothing happens without his permission. If nothing happens without his permission, then everything that happens serves his goal or else he would not have permitted it. God has a reason for his permission or his actions. That reason is his original intent in creation. He wants a people who share his triune fellowship. God, then, permits or causes whatever happens for the sake of this original intent.

This is the key structural principle of God's story in the Bible. Everything God does and permits has this principle at its root. No matter what happens, God intends that whatever happens express this purpose and tend toward that goal.

This yields an important principle. We are often self-absorbed with our own happiness. Everything we do has the goal of happiness. If we are unhappy in our marriage, we get a divorce. If we are unhappy in our work, we change jobs. We expend a great amount of energy in recreation, escapism (drugs and alcohol), and adventures (sexual as well as thrill-seeking) in order to satisfy our deep longings for happiness or to forget our unhappiness. We promote, use, and even distort whatever we possess (power, wealth, fame, knowledge, talents, family, even religion) in the hope that we might find happiness in those things. We are restless until we are happy, and we are unhappy because we are restless.

God's goal for us is happiness, but it is not the kind of happiness which we self-absorbed, fallen humans seek. We seek our own selves, our own autonomy, and our own independence. God's goal, however, is that we find happiness in communion with him. God desires our happiness, but he also, as Creator, has defined it. Happiness is to enjoy God forever.

We are designed for happiness, but we have always looked for it in the wrong places. We seek the creature rather than the Creator. We seek sensual pleasure rather than communion with God. We choose the tangible over the intangible, the seen over the unseen, the temporal over the eternal. We choose ourselves, others, or things over God. We have been looking for love in all the wrong places.

God's response to our misguided search is to initiate redemption. God permits and acts with a view toward accomplishing his goal. He seeks communion with his creatures. Though he dwells in us now through his Holy Spirit (1 Cor. 6:19), he too yearns for a face-to-face communion. Consequently, God is more interested in our communion with him than our sensual pleasure. He calls us to faith and trust.

Therefore, God's intent is not to make everyone happy in the way that we want to be happy (e.g., wealth, fame, power, knowledge). God does not ensure everyone's happiness in the world by providing them with everything their fallen hearts desire. God is not Santa Claus. His ultimate goal is not a temporal happiness, but an eternal one. Consequently, if our temporal pain serves God's eternal goal, then God may very well afflict us with pain because of his priorities. Thus, we may confess with the psalmist that it is "good" to be afflicted (Ps. 119:71). When we recognize the "goodness" of the affliction, we can also recognize its origin. God afflicted the psalmist who confessed: "in faithfulness you have afflicted me" (Ps. 119:75). The faithfulness of God was God's own commitment to his goal. God was more interested in the psalmist's faith than he was his pleasure. Consequently, when it is necessary to accomplish his goal, God may afflict us in order that we might seek him. The affliction may be the very thing that turns us from sensual pursuits to communion with him. This is at least what the psalmist thought when he wrote, "Before I was afflicted I went astray, but now I obey your word" (Ps. 119:67).

> God's response to our misguided search is to initiate redemption.

God uses troubles, tribulations, and trials to generate, strengthen, or refine our faith. God is interested in our faith as a means of communion with him. As a result, he will use whatever means necessary to turn us from unbelief to belief, from distrust to trust; to turn us from the world and its sensual pleasures to the joy of communion with him. God will use the circumstances of this fallen world to accomplish his eternal goal, and this involves the discipline, training, and testing of his people.

> God will use the circumstances of this fallen
> world to accomplish his eternal goal.

"Fairness" must be evaluated in the light of his goal. God is no respector of persons (Acts 10:34) in the sense that he has the same goal for everyone. He yearns for his people and intends that all share in his heavenly communion. God does not want anyone to perish (2 Pet. 3:9). But while God has the same intent for everyone, he may use different means to achieve his goal much like we treat our children differently because they have different personalities and needs. In other words, God is under no obligation to treat everyone just alike in a kind of egalitarian justice. Nor must everyone receive his deserved share of blessings and sufferings in a kind of distributive justice. Egalitarian and distributive justice applied to God's dealings with human beings is more the American democratization of God than it is the biblical story.

God did not treat Ishmael the same way he treated Issac (Gen. 17), and neither did he treat Esau as he treated Jacob (Rom. 9:9-16). God has the sovereign right to treat people differently. He may give wealth to some but poverty to others (1 Sam. 2:7). He may give health to some, but sickness to others. "Fairness" does not mean that God treats everyone exactly the same or with an equal distribution of blessings and sufferings. It only means that he has the same intent for everyone. Consequently, God may use "affliction" to achieve his goal, or he may use "blessing." God disciplines, trains, and tests his people in view of what will best accomplish that goal in any particular situation.

This is climactically demonstrated in Jesus Christ. God willed the death of Jesus in order to redeem a people. God was sovereign over all the events of Jesus' ministry, life and death. It was by "God's set purpose and foreknowledge" that Jesus was handed over to death (Acts 2:23). At any moment the plan could have changed because God was sovereign over the plan. Jesus could have called for "twelve legions of angels," but instead he submitted to the will of the Father (Matt. 26:53). In his sovereignty, God executed a plan for the redemption of a fallen world through Jesus Christ. Yet, this plan involved the suffering and death of the Just One, God's own Son. Nevertheless, because God's goal is communion with his people, God willed the death of his Son out of his great love for us. God sacrificed his own joy so that others might join his fellowship.

> God sacrificed his own joy so that others might join his fellowship.

THE TRUST FACTOR

God seeks a people who seek him. God yearns for a people who love him. God desires a reciprocal relationship of mutual love. God permits or acts in the world in order to maximize the potential of that relationship. He tests, disciplines, redeems, and even punishes to secure the ends of his original intention. God uses the circumstances of a fallen world to serve his ultimate purpose.

God, therefore, is at work in everything for the good of his people (Rom. 8:28). The "good" that God has in mind is not defined by human aspirations of happiness, success, and pleasure. Rather, the "good" that God intends is a conformity to the image of his Son both here and in the heavenly kingdom (Rom. 8:29). God intends a holy communion between himself and his people. If discipline, testing, suffering, or prosperity is necessary toward that end, then that is what God will permit or do.

As a result, I am confident that whatever circumstance befalls me, God has a purpose. God is at work to promote and seek the fulfillment of his original intent for me. God uses every fallen situation for my eternal good. God perfects me through suffering, just as he perfected his own Son through suffering (Heb. 5:7-10). My confidence, then, is that my experience is not the random result of lucky or unlucky coincidences, but it is the work of God in my life to shape me into the image of his Son. God will use everything in my life toward the goal of building my character, shaping my faith, and ushering me into communion with him. And the biblical story tells me that God is so sovereign and so loving that nothing happens in my life that does not serve that end. That is the trust factor. "Our God is in heaven; he does whatever pleases him. . . . O house of Israel, trust in the LORD" (Ps. 115:3,9).

That kind of sovereignty does not frighten me. On the contrary, it comforts me. If God were a malicious tyrant, I would be terrified. But God has demonstrated his love, care and empathy. I have reason to trust him. God's sovereignty, then, emboldens my faith, grounds my contentment, and enables me to submit to God's

God's sovereignty emboldens my faith, grounds my contentment, and enables me to submit to God's purposes.

purposes in the fallen circumstances of my life. God's sovereignty plus his care means that I trust that whatever happens in my life serves the eternal good that God intends for me. I may not understand, but I do trust.

CONCLUSION

God's sovereignty means that he will use all his resources to accomplish his goal. He will do whatever it takes to achieve the purpose he has for his people. This means his love will go all the way to the cross. This means his empathy will share every pain. And it means that he will discipline, refine, test, punish, and bless his people for the sake of that goal.

God is more interested in my faith than he is my pleasure. He is more interested in a mutual communion than he is my health and prosperity. In faithfulness to his goal and out of his great love, God will afflict his people if it serves his goal. God is at work in everything for good, and he works out of his love, empathy, and faithfulness.

Despite the dire circumstances of the world and despite the fact that we are surrounded by fallenness, the people of God must learn to trust the sovereign love of God. Who else will we trust?

Reflecting on Lesson Seven

1. What do you find most problematic about divine sovereignty?

2. What does it mean to say that God controls or reigns over trouble? Does that disturb you? Why?

3. Was God responsible for Job's trouble? Why do you think so? Why did God not end his trouble sooner than he did? Was God not sovereign over the trouble?

4. What is God's goal for his creation?

5. What do you think about the statement, "God must treat everyone just alike"? Is it fair for God to give one person poverty and another prosperity?

6. What is God's motive in discipline and his activity in the world?

7. Can you believe that God is at work in everything that happens in your life?

8. Describe a circumstance in your life where you believe God's hand was particularly visible. What was God doing with your life at that moment?

Consider this:

If you have suffered the loss of a loved one, the pain is very real whether or not you are a believer. If you are a believer, explain how the promised resurrection changes your grief. If you are not a believer, what would be your greatest wish for your lost one? For your future?

8

ANCHOR FIVE:
THE ULTIMATE VICTORY OF GOD

In this lesson:
- ▶ The mercy of God's deliverance
- ▶ The ultimate victory over death (and suffering) through resurrection
- ▶ Our final dwelling place with God

Then I saw a new heaven and a new earth, for the first heaven and the first
earth had passed away, and there was no longer any sea. I saw the Holy
City, the new Jerusalem, coming down out of heaven from God, prepared as
a bride beautifully dressed for her husband. And I heard a loud voice
from the throne saying, "Now the dwelling of God is with men,
and he will live with them. They will be his people,
and God himself will be with them and be their God. He will wipe

every tear from their eyes. There will be no more death or mourning or crying or pain, for the old order of things has passed away.

—Revelation 21:1-4

The fifth anchor for the soul is the ultimate victory of God. Death destroys hope. The grave looks so final, so irreversible. This world is so full of hate, sin, and suffering that it appears irredeemable.

But God's work is not yet done. God will one day act to reverse the curse, raise the dead, and renew the earth. God has given us a glimpse of this victory in Jesus Christ, but we still wait for its fuller revelation. We wait for the fullness of God's heavenly kingdom where the promise quoted above will be fulfilled.

DIVINE DELIVERANCE

"Your kingdom come, your will be done on earth as it is in heaven" (Matt. 6:10). These familiar words express a yearning for the end-time. They are a cry for the consummation, the heavenly kingdom, where there will be no more pain, tears, and death. It has been the prayer of God's people since the Fall. From the beginning promise that one day the seed of the woman would crush the head of the serpent (Gen. 3:15) to the closing act of Revelation where the apostle prays "Come, Lord Jesus" (Rev. 22:20), the people of God have expected the fullness of God's reign in the world. They pray that God would fully implement his reign over the world, destroy his enemies, and live among his people.

The prayer for the consummation is the cry of God's oppressed people for deliverance from the bondage of death. One day God will answer this cry and reveal his heavenly kingdom (2 Tim. 4:1). While that kingdom has not yet come, God has revealed his intention through various mighty acts within redemptive history. When Israel cried out to God under the burden of their slavery, God heard them, came near, and delivered them through Moses (Exod. 2:23-25; Num. 20:16; Deut. 26:7; 1 Sam. 12:8). When Israel cried out to God during their oppression under the King of Aram, God heard them, came near, and delivered them through Othniel (Judg. 3:8-9). When Israel cried out to God during their oppression under the Midianites, God heard them, came near, and delivered them through Gideon (Judg. 6:7-12). When Israel cried out to God during their oppression under the Philistines, God heard them, came near, and delivered them through Samuel (1 Sam. 7:5-11). When individuals within Israel's history cried out to the Lord in their distress, God heard them, came near, and redeemed them from their troubles (Ps. 18:6; 34:6; 40:1; 107:13,19; 145:19). This pattern of oppression-cry-deliverance is the cycle of fall and redemption. The

> The people of God fall, they are oppressed by their sin, and then they turn to God who answers them.

people of God fall, they are oppressed by their sin, and then they turn to God who answers them through his redemptive work. Nehemiah recalls this gracious pattern: "And when they cried out to you again, you heard from heaven, and in your compassion you delivered them time after time" (Neh. 9:28).

This theme is carried into the New Testament as well. It appears in Luke where the birth of Jesus is understood as God's remembrance of Israel (Luke 1:54-55,72-75). Jesus is announced as the one who will reign forever and his kingdom will never end (Luke 1:32-33). The prophet of the Most High, John the Baptist, will "give light to those who sit in darkness and in the shadow of death" (Luke 1:79, NRSV). God has remembered his people in order to rescue Israel from the hands of its enemies (Luke 1:74). Mark announces a new Exodus through the prophet John. God will make a way through the wilderness (Mark 1:2-3). This is the good news of the kingdom of God (Mark 1:14-15). Matthew announces that Jesus comes to bring light to darkness and to deliver God's people from the shadows of death (Matt. 4:15-17). Quoting Isaiah 9:1-2, Matthew interprets the ministry of Jesus as God's mighty act of redemption for the oppressed. Through the ministry of Jesus, God breaks the back of the oppressor as he did in the day of Midian (Isa. 9:4). Jesus will sit on the throne of David and there will be no end to his kingdom (Isa. 9:6-7).

In the ministry of Jesus Christ, then, God reveals his kingdom, and he acts to destroy the oppressor. He heals the lame, blind, and sick; exorcises demons; and destroys death (Matt. 11:4-6; Luke 4:18-19). It is good news for the oppressed. Jesus hears the cries of the oppressed, the hurting, and sick, and he answers their cry with compassionate redemption. When two blind men cried out for mercy, Jesus heard them and healed them (Matt. 9:27-31). When the father of the demoniac cried out for help, Jesus heard him and exorcised the demon (Mark 9:24). As Jesus proclaimed the "good news of the kingdom," he also cured "every disease and sickness" (Matt. 9:35). In his ministry of compassion, healing, and proclamation, Jesus "took our infirmities and bore our diseases" (Matt. 8:14-17, NRSV). The ministry of Jesus is God's answer to the cry of fallen humanity who seek release from the power of Satan, sin, and death.

> The ministry of Jesus is God's answer to the cry of fallen humanity.

This is epitomized in the cry of the one who not only suffered with us but also suffered for us. In the Garden, his tears expressed his anguish, and his voice cried out to his Father for deliverance (Luke 22:39-46). His Father heard his cry and delivered him. He asked for a way out, and when he submitted to the Father's will, he cried on the cross, "My God, My God, why have you forsaken me?" (Matt. 27:46 quoting Ps. 22:1). God heard his cry. The writer of Hebrews notes, "During the days of Jesus' life on earth, he offered up prayers and petitions with loud cries and tears to the one who could save him from death, and he was heard because of his reverent submission" (5:7). The pattern of God's history with his people is repeated: the faithful cry out, God hears, and God delivers. Psalm 22 reflects this same pattern. The cry of verse 1, and the anguish of the first few verses ("I am a worm," 22:6), are answered by God. Just as God had answered the cries of his people in the past when they trusted him (22:4-5), so God answered the cry of this faithful one (Ps. 22:22-24).

God heard the cry of Jesus, and he answered him. God delivered him through resurrection. God did not leave his holy one in Hades, but he raised him from the dead. In this remembrance, in this act of resurrection, God reveals that "dominion belongs to" him (Ps. 22:28). God has acted to destroy Satan, sin, and death. God has declared victory in the resurrection of Jesus.

Now the people of God wait for the fullness of that victory. Just as the souls under the altar "called out in a loud voice" with their lament of "how long?" (Rev. 6:10), so we wait with our groanings, tears, and cries for the consummation. We wait for the final revelation of God's kingdom. We wait for the time when, like Israel, God will take note of our groaning, hear our cry, and send his Son one more time to reveal his heavenly kingdom. Our confidence is that just as God has acted in the past for Israel, and just as he acted in the resurrection of Jesus, so he will act on our behalf when his Son returns.

93   Trusting God in the Storms of Life

DEATH AND RESURRECTION

Death is the epitome of fallenness. It covers the whole human race. Everyone, including children, are subject to death's dominion. This is the reverse of what God intended. God did not create so that his people would die. The opposite is true. God created for life, communion, and fellowship. Death is an alien invader. Sin created death, and as far as sin reigns, death reigns.

However, God will not let death win. Death will not claim the final victory. Rather, God's intent for his creation will find fruition in an eternal reality, in a new heaven and a new earth. There God will plant the tree of life by the water of life and there will be no more curse (Rev. 22:1-5). There we will see the face of God and experience the fullness of his presence. There God will fulfill his original intent in creation and dwell among his people. In that place there will be no more pain, death, or mourning because God will wipe away every tear (Rev. 21:1-4). Everything fallen will be renewed; everything old will become new. God will dwell among his people eternally.

In the present circumstance, where death has dominion, it is difficult to believe in God's eternal reality.

But in the present circumstance, where death has dominion, it is difficult to believe that God will ultimately bring about that eternal reality. When we stand by the coffin of our loved one, it is difficult to envision or even trust in that new heaven and new earth. Death so dominates us that faith is difficult. Death looks like a closed door that no one can open. Death conquers hope.

For this reason God entered history in Jesus Christ to demonstrate his future victory over death. God demonstrated his power over death in the resurrection of Jesus (1 Cor. 15:12-18). Indeed, the resurrection of Jesus is an end-time act itself. It is an event that comes from the future. Jesus is the firstfruit of an end-time harvest. Jesus is the first resurrection of a resurrection harvest (1 Cor. 15:21-28). God has given us a taste of the future in the resurrection of Jesus. God has shown us what the future is like. He has shown us what the end of history is. *Resurrected life is the end of history.* Resurrection conquers death. The only real question about the end of history is whether God will find a people who wait for him in faith (Luke 18:8). God has testified about his future work — he will raise the dead. But what is our testimony to God — will we wait in faith?

> God has given us a taste of the future in the resurrection of Jesus.

Death does not conquer hope in the eyes of faith. In the resurrection of Jesus God has given us eyes to see the destruction of death. We still grieve, but we do not grieve without hope (1 Thess. 4:13-18). We still experience loss, but we know that we will regain what was lost. We still lament, but we trust in God's sovereignty over death.

NEW HEAVEN AND NEW EARTH

God has always wanted to dwell among his people where he can be their God and they can be his people (cf. Gen. 17:7; Lev. 26:11-12; Jer. 24:7; 32:38; Ezek. 36:28; Zech. 8:8; 2 Cor. 6:16; Rev. 21:3). The promise of God is that we will be with him "forever." This is the central hope of God's people, that is, that God will be present among them. To dwell in the house of the Lord forever is the singular hope of God's people, and it is a hope that will find fulfillment when Jesus returns. Then we will see the face of God and dwell with him forever (Rev. 22:1-5).

> To dwell in the house of the Lord forever is the singular hope of God's people.

However, the "new earth" will be a very different one than the one we now inhabit. Sin, corruption, decay, tears, and death will no longer fill it. The old earth with its age-old problems will have passed away and a new earth will have arrived "for the old order of things has passed away" (Rev. 21:4). We will live with the Lord in a new heaven and a new earth where everything old and fallen will be renewed and restored (Rev. 21:1-4). This new heaven and new earth will be the home of the righteous (2 Pet. 3:13).

God will redeem creation itself, just as he will redeem our souls and our bodies (cf. Rom. 8:23). God's redemption is cosmic in character (Col. 1:20 — things in heaven and things on the earth). He will turn everything back to its original purpose, both things in heaven and things on the earth. Just as he will redeem fallen bodies through resurrection, so he will redeem the fallen creation through re-creation just as he now transforms us through his Holy Spirit (Rom. 8:19-23).

The creation, including our bodies, was subjected to the futility and bondage of a fallen world. God subjected the world to frustration in the hope of liberating the creation from its bondage. Because of the fall, our bodies die, we grieve, and we suffer. This world, full of sin and disease, is not the world God created. God will judge this world, and in the flaming fire of vengeance he will destroy those rebels who continue in their sinful refusal to acknowledge and obey him (2 Thess. 1:7-9). But God's redemptive intent is to renew the world just as he intends to redeem our bodies. God will create a new heaven and a new earth (Rev. 21:1-4; 2 Pet. 3:13; cf. Isa. 65:17; 66:22). God will make his dwelling place among humankind in a new heaven and new earth, in a new city, in a new Eden, and in that garden there will be no more curse. There will be no more pain, no more tears, and no more death (Rev. 21:1-4; 22:1-5). Through the work of Christ, God reverses the fall and renews the earth. He redeems us from our sins and resurrects our dead bodies. Once again, God will live among his people just as he did in the

> Through the work of Christ, God reverses the fall and renews the earth.

Garden of Eden. The original intention of God's creative work will be fulfilled through his redemption of the fallen creation.

Sometimes our view of heaven is too other-worldly. We think that heaven is some ethereal, almost surreal, place somewhere in the sky. We think heaven is out-there, over-there, or some-where other than here. Certainly, here and now is not heaven — it is far from it. This place is full of sin, death, mourning, tears, and pain. But this is not what God created. He created Eden where the voice of God was heard in the midst of the garden; where harmony, peace, and joy were experienced throughout creation; where God communed with his newly created human community. One day, God will destroy this fallen earth and redeem it so that his saints might inhabit a new earth. There we will live with God forever. It is described as a great city — the size of the Mediterranean Sea (Rev. 21:9-27). It is described as a wed-ding celebration between Christ and his church. It is described as a new heaven and a new earth. Sin destroyed this world, but God will renew it. Heaven is not out-there or over-there. Heaven is where God will dwell with his saints forever, and he will dwell with them on a new heaven and a new earth.

CONCLUSION

I do not, of course, relish the moment of my son's death. My lament continues, and I expect my grief will intensify as that moment grows closer. In fact, I yearn for the quick return of the Lord. I want him to come now. I do not want to watch my son wither away and die. I want that resurrection life for him now, and I want it for all sufferers. I want to hear Joshua say, "I love you" again. I want to see him run and play. I want, well, what I want is death destroyed. I want the eternal reality now! So, I pray, "Your kingdom come!" So, I pray, "*Maranatha*" (1 Cor. 16:22). So I pray, and so I trust, and so I wait.

While this reminder is important and it offers the substance of hope for the believer, it does not dispel the grief of a parent. We still grieve because we have truly lost something. We may grieve with hope, but we still grieve. What we want is no longer here. Our dreams have been destroyed. We will not see our children's children (cf. Ps. 128:6). The resurrection means we grieve in a different manner than those who grieve without hope, but it does not dissipate the grief because what was lost in the present is still lost. The loss is not regained until the end of time. But the hope of restoration comforts believers.

God has given us hope in Jesus Christ, and through faith we patiently wait for his eternal kingdom (Rom. 8:18-23).

Reflecting on Lesson Eight

1. In what ways was the ministry of Jesus a light in the darkness? How did his ministry anticipate the fullness of the heavenly kingdom? What happened in his ministry that is like the new heaven and new earth?

2. Should we pray for the consummation? Should we pray for the second coming of Jesus and the fullness of his kingdom? Why is that important? What does praying for the coming kingdom enable our hearts to express?

3. What does it mean to say that death is the epitome of fallenness? What does it mean to say that death is God's enemy?

4. How does the resurrection of Jesus testify to our own resurrection?

5. What is the new heaven and the new earth? What is important about that image for sufferers? How does it provide comfort?

6. What does it mean to "grieve with hope"? What is the nature of the grief? What is the nature of the hope? Should we counsel people to stop weeping at the grave because of the resurrection? Why must grief still express itself even when there is a hope of the resurrection?

Consider this:

When tragedies enter our lives, the pain is horribly real. No magic wand or carefully followed formula can remove that pain. We cannot wipe it from our own lives, and we cannot exorcise it from one we love who is hurting. What good is it, then, to discuss how God works or does not work within these events and in our lives? Does it make a difference to know that God is ultimately good and that he has our best interests at heart? How has this study helped you to better understand pain? Will you be able to more effectively support others when they suffer? Can you trust God now more than you could before you began this study?

Option 2

These five anchors can only be a real comfort to those who have put their trust in God and Jesus and who believe the promises they have given us. If you are hurting, are you willing to trust God? If you are comforting a loved one, do they have a relationship with God? Without this, your efforts to bring comfort may be futile.

CONCLUSION

Praise be to the God and Father of our Lord Jesus Christ, who has blessed us in the heavenly realms with every spiritual blessing in Christ. For he chose us in him before the creation of the world to be holy and blameless in his sight. In love he predestined us to be adopted as his sons through Jesus Christ, in accordance with his pleasure and will—

—Ephesians 1:3-5

Now faith is being sure of what we hope for and certain of what we do not see. . . . And without faith it is impossible to please God, because anyone who comes to him must believe that he exists and that he rewards those who earnestly seek him.

—Hebrews 11:1,6

These five anchors are theocentric — focused on what God has done. But they are also Christocentric — demonstrated in

Jesus Christ. This is God's story. It is what God has done. It is how God has loved, how he has cared, and what he has willed to do. It is God's story *in* Jesus Christ. The story of Jesus is the climax of the biblical story. It is the story of God's love, care, empathy, sovereignty, and victory for us. The story of Jesus is the story of God.

God loves us, and he has demonstrated this at the cross. God listens to us, and he responds with his comforting presence. God understands us, and he himself experienced fallenness through suffering in Jesus Christ. God orchestrates the world for us, and he sovereignly rules it so that it serves his ultimate goal. God will destroy death and fallenness for us, and he has demonstrated this in the resurrection of Jesus Christ.

These reminders are revealed in Jesus Christ. This is the message of the gospel. It is good news. God has given us an indubitable testimony of himself in Jesus Christ. Whatever doubts, fears, confusions, and questions may surround us, the incarnation, ministry, cross, and resurrection of Jesus testify to God's redemption. In Jesus Christ God has shown us who he is and what he will do. That testimony assails all doubts and comforts all questions.

God loves. God listens. God understands. God rules. God wins. This is the ground and substance of faith. It enables us to endure suffering, and it empowers faith. It is the substance of God's story among his people, and God's story gives faith its confidence.